CHRISTIANITY
DEBUGGED

Table of Contents

Introduction

Over the past nearly 2000 years, Christianity has picked up what computer people call "bugs," trash of various kinds that compromises and prevents the working of the computer and may include a "worm" that slowly and progressively eats up its vital parts. Christianity has become like a computer that has lots of stuff in it that does not belong in it and has spiritual "worms" eating it up. It is very badly damaged. Bible translations, churches, traditions and traditional beliefs, and religious preachers and teachers prevent Jesus from leading and teaching his people. They misdirect multitudes.

The Israelites with Moses refused God's offer to them to individually obey God's voice and be His "kingdom of priests" (Ex. 19:5,6, Ex. 20:19). They wanted Moses to speak to them in place of God speaking to each of them personally (Ex. 20:19). God allowed that and let them go into bondage under rules and regulations enforced by men. They demanded a king which God allowed; and He let them destroy themselves (Hos. 13:9,11).

So it is in Christianity. Men are refusing to be "a kingdom of priests;" and now God has not offered them anything else (I Pet. 2:5,9, Rev. 1:6, 5:10). God has torn open the temple curtain that kept Israelites from Him (Mt. 27:51). Each person is to know God for himself or herself in the New Covenant (Heb. 8:11, Jer. 31:33,34). God has said "I will dwell IN them and walk IN them" (II Cor. 6:16). Paul wrote: "For it is God which works IN you both to will and to do of His good pleasure" (Phil. 2:13). Jesus said his sheep each hear his voice and follow him (Jn. 10:27,28). John wrote that we should "walk [live, behave] even as he [Jesus] walked" (I Jn. 2:6). Only "as many as are led by the Spirit of God" are "the sons of God" (Rom. 8:14). Jesus prayed that in the same way as he and God were in each other, we would be in them now (Jn. 17:21-23).

Anything else is **wrong and not what Jesus has for us.** But again, men are ignoring God and destroying themselves and fighting those who speak truth from God. Many churches look good but are infested with ungodly men and practices. Their leaders mislead them. They teach them to appear godly to men but

1

do not teach them to be good to God. Leaders often are hirelings whose jobs depend on cooperation with ungodly people.

While disease has not fully killed Christianity, the enemy within it has paralyzed most of it. It has a lot of men's ideas and practices that are thought to be sacred but are actually ungodly and very destructive. They give temporary rewards and solutions that may reduce pain and give excitement and help; but they cover up the roots of the problems men face.

Much of the pollution that is in Christian churches, teachings, and Bible translations was introduced toward the end of the first century. After that there were more and more changes until now authentic Christianity is nearly extinct. Jesus, as recorded in Revelation chapters 2 and 3, addresses the ungodly heresies and practices in 6 apparently first century churches in "Asia" (Turkey). Jesus said the church at Sardis was dead, the one at Laodicea was spiritually blind and nauseated him, the church at Ephesus had lost its first love (of obeying and abiding in him), 2 churches had false ruinous teachings and teachers, one had a little strength and an opportunity to grow, and only one church, a seventh church that was at Smyrna, was faithful and spiritually rich.

When you see and reject the stuff that is preventing Christ's living in you and guiding you personally, as well as is injuring multitudes of others, you can be set free to participate in the activity of authentic Christianity.

When you do not muster the fortitude to reject and give up the "worms" and "viruses" and choose truth, you are enslaved to traditions that will keep you from knowing God and participating in Christ. You also will mislead others.

No one can take the place of the anointing that God has sent that "teaches you of all things" so that you "need not that any man teach you" (I Jn. 2:27). Leaders often usurp the Holy Spirit's job and prevent the New Covenant in which God directly writes His laws in <u>individual</u> minds and hearts and each <u>individual</u> is knowing God for himself (Heb. 8:10,11). You will die or are already dead spiritually if you tolerate men coming between you and God. They cripple you and intimidate you. Jesus has come through the baptism in the Holy Spirit to teach and deliver rewards not to just leaders, but to equally administrate God to each person and live in and give life abundantly in each one who receives Holy Spirit baptism and seeks and lives to Jesus.

God has given "great and precious promises that by these you might be partakers of the divine nature" (II Pet. 1:4). These guarantees are to each and every individual. God has enabled each individual to know God for himself or herself. He has promised to give wisdom to <u>anyone</u> who is asking and waiting for the answer (Ja. 1:5-8, Mt. 7:8). Jesus said that "everyone that asks receives, and he that seeks finds, and to him that knocks it shall be opened" (Mt. 7:8). Many leaders oppose that God's promises are as much to you the individual as to them. Some leaders will try to rob you from having a precious relationship with your heavenly Father. They want you to believe God will talk to you only through them and that you need them and need to honor them. If they succeed in convincing you that they are vital to you and you cannot know and hear God for yourself, they have won and you are their captives believing in the handicap they claim you have. They have "dumbed" you down.

If you are truly seeking God, you will be willing to take actions to obey Him; otherwise you are just looking and perhaps hoping to confirm what you already believe. If you are truly seeking, you will be finding and being changed.

This book may help you understand some things; but it is only if you are seeking God and truth that you will be receiving spiritually from God (Mt. 7:7,8). Seeking is a major and continual activity in Christianity. You must act on what God shows if you want God to show you more.

Your wholehearted seeking will prepare and make your heart to be a receptacle for hearing God. You alone must do that. God will honor Mt. 7:8 and Ja. 1:5-8 and answer you when you are seeking Him; however, you may find that you need to seek much more and longer than you had thought would be necessary. Jesus tells you that **you** have to "find" (or "be finding") the way that is leading to spiritual life, and "few" "find" it (Mt. 7:14). But if you follow Jesus' command to keep seeking, it is guaranteed you will find (Mt. 7:8). God says in Jer. 29:13: "And you shall seek Me, and find Me, when you shall search for Me with all your heart." Acts 17:27,28 says God put men on earth to be seeking and finding Him and that it is "in Him we live and move and have our being."

3

The "worms" and "viruses" in Christianity are attractive to immature men and <u>carnally motivated</u> men. That is why God has given us a Shepherd , scriptures, and the Holy Spirit so we can be guided "into all truth" (Jn. 16:13) and be knowing the truth and having the truth setting each of us free (Jn. 8:32). Without Jesus' present leading and participation in his body, the church, and in us individually, our failures are guaranteed by God Who sent us a savior. Men must ask and get God's directions and help or they will live in delusions.

Over time, what has become strong in Christianity is what is not Christianity. The worst has come to the top. Much of it is just a false substitute, what in Biblical Greek is called "antichrist" teaching. The worst of it is welcomed by "the many there be which go in" "the wide" "gate" and "broad" "way" "that leads to destruction" (Mt. 7:13). They follow orthodox teachings, dead traditions and various leaders instead of God's Word, Jesus and the Holy Spirit.

This book is written for true seekers who are willing to be acting on what Jesus is **showing them**. For participating Christians, the door is open and the adventure is fantastic. It is your place to take hold of the opportunity God is giving you individually and to press on into greater and greater experience of His life in you and into the wisdom, truth and activities that make you, like Jesus, to be in the image and likeness of God. Real Christianity is taking advantage of the opportunity to **press into** God's kingdom (Lk. 16:16).

Participation in God's kingdom will involve you being changed from glory to glory into a son of God like Jesus. You mature and become spiritually minded but die to being just naturally minded. The adventure and challenge dwarfs all others.

Translations used here are identified if they are not from the *King James Version*. At times, some words will be changed into modern English as the *New King James Version* and others do. Present tenses and future tenses may be translated in the continuous sense, which is alternate correct translation. For instance, you would read that the "pure [single-minded] in heart will be seeing God" rather than that the "pure in heart will see God."

4

Various "bugs" will be dealt with throughout this book. Many objections that will arise in your mind will be dealt with as you read on. We cannot deal with all the "bugs" we are targeting simultaneously. Preconceptions and misconceptions are not easily dislodged; however, if you persevere, "the truth shall make you free" (Jn. 8:32). Jesus promises it. He also said that the reason he was "born" and "came" "unto the world" is to "bear witness unto the truth" (Jn. 18:37).

The experience God has for you is unique. This writer is going through unique and wonderful experiences. Some give him fear and trembling as he goes where he has never been before. Some are fantastic and mind boggling. That is the way life with God is. We are all invited. Some hear God and are not just invited to participate in His will: they are commanded and obligated. May your journey be one of rich experience with God and with those who live in Him.

This book is intended to clear the way for men to "worship in spirit and in truth." Jesus said "they that worship Him [God] must worship Him [God] in spirit and in truth" and that "true worshippers shall worship the Father in spirit and in truth" (Jn. 4:24,23).

1

What Did Jesus and His Apostles Preach?

Let us start by remembering that Jesus said he "MUST preach the kingdom of God...for therefore am I sent" (Lk. 4:43). That is what Jesus preached and what God sent him to preach. God's wants to give us the kingdom (Lk. 12:30).

After John's imprisonment, Jesus "came into Galilee preaching the gospel of the kingdom of God" (Mk. 1:14). Jesus went "throughout every city and village preaching and showing the glad tidings of the kingdom of God" (Lk. 8:1). Jesus "went about all the cities and villages teaching in their synagogues and preaching the gospel [good news] of the kingdom" (Mt. 9:35, Mt. 4:23). Jesus sent his apostles "to preach the kingdom of God" (Lk. 9:2). Jesus told a follower, a man who wanted to stay with his father until he died and was buried, that he should let the dead bury their dead: but that the follower was to "go and preach the kingdom of God" (Lk. 9:59,60). Jesus said that "the law and the prophets were until John: since that time the kingdom of God is preached and **every** man presses into it [the kingdom of God]" (Lk.16:16). He told us to make it our "first" priority to be seeking "the kingdom of God [God ruling in us] and His righteousness [His right ways, the ways of the kingdom]" (Mt. 6:33).

John the Dipper (Baptist, Baptizer) had come saying: "Repent [change your thinking and what you are doing], for the kingdom of God is at hand [has drawn near]" (Mt. 3:2). Jesus had first begun "to preach and to say: 'Repent: for the kingdom of heaven is at hand' " (Mt. 4:17). The first thing for which Jesus told his disciples to ask when they prayed was: "Thy kingdom come" (Mt. 6:10). In the "Sermon on the Mount," when it is translated literally, Jesus says the reign of the heavens, "the kingdom of heaven," is of those who are impoverished or "poor" in spirit (Mt. 5:3): and he says that the kingdom of the heavens is of them that are persecuted because of their doing and standing for righteousness, the ways of the kingdom of God (Mt. 5:10).

Joseph of Arimathaea "waited for the kingdom of God" (Mk. 15:43).

After Jesus rose from his grave, he appeared to his apostles during 40 days "speaking of the things pertaining to the kingdom of God" (Acts 1:3).

Philip went up to Samaria and was believed by the Samaritans concerning his "preaching the things concerning the kingdom of God and the name of Jesus Christ" (Acts 8:12). Paul went into the Ephesian synagogue "and spoke boldly for the space of 3 months, disputing and persuading the things concerning the kingdom of God" (Acts 19:8). He later spoke to the Ephesian church elders and declared what he had been ministering to them: "I know that you all among whom I have gone **preaching the kingdom of God**, shall see my face no more" (Acts 20:25). "Paul dwelt two whole years in his own hired house…preaching the kingdom of God and teaching those things which concern the Lord Jesus Christ" (Acts 28:30,31). Jesus said: "this gospel of the kingdom shall be preached in all the world for a witness to all nations: and then shall the end come" (Mt. 24:14).

So why do most of the churches not teach the things concerning the kingdom of God? Why do they preach anything else? Are there religious spirits blinding men so that they tolerate being captivated by vain religion rather than by knowing Jesus and God themselves (Jn. 17:3)?

Why is it that the gospel of the kingdom of God, God's kingdom in men, is not the gospel (good news) to them? How is it that Jesus said that now "the kingdom of God is preached and every man presses into it" (Lk. 16:16) but we do not see any such thing being preached or pressed into? How come? Why not? Is major orthodox traditional Christianity outrageously crippled with phony deceptive teaching or "bugs"? Is it obscured by fake salvation? How come most all "gospel [good news]" that is preached now consists of the morbid fear of hell and the promise of heaven in the hereafter rather than the glorious opportunity to enter or be entering and participating in God's kingdom, His business, now and here? How did the switch come about? Why do the big denominations not tell us that a Christian's "citizenship is in heaven" (Phil. 3:20 A.S.V.), that we are a kingdom of God's **priests** (I Pet. 2:5,9, Rev. 1:6, 5:10) and we are raised up to be in union with Jesus "in heavenly places" now (Eph. 2:6)? Why do they invent fictitious problems and then invent their solutions?

8

Do they not know that participation in the kingdom of God is real and is for here and now and is what Christianity is about? Do they not know that the kingdom of God is what Jesus lived and taught and what his apostles lived and taught and that God sent Jesus to preach the kingdom of God? Do they not know that living in the kingdom of God here and now is the greatest adventure, challenge, opportunity, rewarding experience and life that a man can be having on this planet? Do they not know that they are doing the devil's deceptive job by misleading multitudes from the gospel, the good news that Jesus preached and also revealed directly to Paul (Gal. 1:12) who said: "If any man preach any other gospel unto you than that you have received, let him be accursed [or "laid on the altar as a sacrifice"]" (Gal. 1:9)? So why do they preach any other? Why do men tolerate anything else?

The answer is simple. The churches are wrongly building kingdoms of their own and they do not want God's kingdom. The kingdom of God is God's directly leading, teaching, dwelling in, fellowshipping with and shepherding each of His people without there being any human spiritual fathers or priests or popes or pastors or rulers except "the man Christ Jesus" (I Tim. 2:5) between His people and Himself. Jesus is the "Shepherd and Bishop of" each of our "souls" (I Pet. 2:25; Jn. 10:27,28); and we can commit spiritual suicide by choosing to believe that Jesus delegates his responsibility rather than that "there is one mediator between God and men, the man Christ Jesus" (I Tim. 2:5). God has cut out all the middle men except Jesus who is in Him so that we can be free to know God and participate in Him ourselves; however, men tragically demand middlemen and refuse to be responsibly hearing and dealing with God for themselves. The Israelites demanded Aaron make them gods. He made a calf of gold (Ex. 32:1-4): men now, in idolatry, make priests and bow down to them, follow fables, and refuse to each be a priest of God.

The churches ignore I Tim. 2:5 and also that the Holy Spirit is to directly guide and teach and comfort each Christian without the aid of some appointed or any "ordained" leader. Churches are keeping God out of their affairs and pretending to be doing His affairs. They want no interference from God. They do not want a mention of His controlling kingdom as being INSIDE people here and now. They hijack Christians from their priesthood

9

and citizenship IN God; and they convince them that God has designated church leaders as their shepherds, thinkers, rulers and intermediaries between men and God. A person's being directed by God, "led by the Spirit of God" (Rom. 8:14), following the Shepherd Jesus (Jn. 10:27,28), is as popular with them as a barn fire in a straw hut.

Jesus was crucified by the church, its theologians, translators and authorities that existed when Jesus was on earth. Christian churches, theologians and translators have been crucifying and destroying Jesus' message for nearly 2000 years since their predecessors killed Jesus. They have been changing it and been irresponsible, dishonest and arrogant in translating scripture. They reject Jesus as Lord.

They also crucify, persecute and destroy those who love the truth and live in it. Jesus said: "Wherefore, behold, I send unto you prophets, and wise men, and scribes [translators, scholars]: and some of them you shall kill and crucify, and some of them shall you scourge in your synagogues [churches] and persecute them from city to city" (Mt. 23:34). "All that will live godly in Christ Jesus shall suffer persecution" (II Tim. 3:12). "...whosoever kills you will think that he does God service" (Jn. 16:2).

Churches and their organizations are willingly ignorant or ignorantly ignorant; however, they are building their own kingdoms and do not want God's interference with their kingdoms any more than the Jewish leaders wanted Jesus and the kingdom of God. Churches before and after Jesus' earthly ministry have wanted to run their own kingdoms without interference from God. Jesus said: "From the days of John the Baptist until now the kingdom of heaven suffers violence, AND THE VIOLENT TAKE IT BY FORCE" (Mt. 11:12), such "force" as titles conferred by men, deceptive teachings, theological degrees bestowed by men with theological degrees, charisma, politics, money, conspiracy, Satan's contributions, and collusion. That is the message of the Parable of God's Vineyard where workers in a man's vineyard refused to allow him any fruit out of his vineyard and determined to kill his son, the heir of the vineyard, so they could own the vineyard (Mt. 21:33-41).

If the gospel of the kingdom of God was the central message shared in the big churches and denominations, the churches would be unrecognizable in contrast to what they are now. And they do not want that to transpire. That is their worst nightmare: that God's kingdom should thrive, that men's spiritual eyes and ears should be opened (Mt. 13:15,16, Acts 28:27), and that men should directly participate with Jesus as priests in the kingdom of God.

Because influential men have chosen man-made gospels and made the false gospels popular, theologians have been left searching for sense in nonsense. They have been led into and are looking up dead end allies and expecting to find passage ways to light and life where there are none. They have been "barking up the wrong tree," as the old expression goes. They have departed from the living gospel of the kingdom of God. And they have come up with all manner of nonsense that a child would refuse if he were not brainwashed and held by fear.

They fail to see that they are rejecting God when they choose traditions and neglect truths in God's word, however unpopular God's word is. Jesus said: "But in vain they do worship me, teaching for doctrines the commandments of men" (Mt. 15:9). They use scriptures and teachings not to help people live to Jesus and God but to further themselves. There is a lot of vain worship disguised as real worship. The Israelites bowed down to idols; "Christians" often choose to do the same.

Medicine was kept in darkness for a thousand years by the teaching of a renowned expert who said the blood was pumped out of the heart and then sucked back into it. Wrong tradition killed many when it was thought that a surgeon was experienced and wise if he entered the operating room with dirty, bloody hands. The idea that the world was flat was held, by prestigious men, to be unquestionable for hundreds of years. George Washington was bled to death in an attempt to cure arthritis by traditional methods. The idea that the earth runs in an orbit around the sun rather than the sun running around the earth was rejected for over a thousand years. The errors among theological philosophers and translators have met the test of time and plunged Christians into darkness and delusions.

We must choose Jesus' gospel and be pressing into the kingdom of God or be misdirected by the traditional gospels. Our outcome will be (1) what God has intended for us or (2) the product of our imaginations and of our being led like cattle on leashes tied to rings in their noses. Either we individually live to God, or we refuse to serve God and choose delusions rather than the kingdom of God.

2

The Kingdom of God

A kingdom is the domain of a king. It is where the king rules. If you are being ruled by God who is <u>in</u> Jesus our Shepherd and Lord and king (Jn. 10:27,28, Lk. 6:46, Lk. 1:32), then you are in God's kingdom or domain. If you are not being ruled by God *in you,* then you are not in God's kingdom. If you live to yourself and your understandings, you will miss God's kingdom. God's kingdom is "righteousness, peace and joy <u>in the Holy Ghost</u>" (Rom. 14:17). It is participation (Gr. *koinonia*) "with the Father and with His Son Jesus Christ" and with those who are also participating with them (I Jn. 1:3,7) so that the participants are "members one of another" (Rom. 12:5, Eph. 4:25).

The kingdom of God cannot be received or entered unless a person is seeking with curiosity and the humble lack of presumption such as small children have (Lk. 18:17, Mk. 10:15). Rich men in the "prosperity doctrine" have about no chance of entering God's kingdom (Mt. 19:24).

What percentage of your effort, time and money are you putting into living to, seeking, and obeying Christ and our heavenly Father? What percentage are you in God's kingdom? What percentage of your efforts are those of pressing into the kingdom of God? God watches percentages and we should too. Jesus said of a poor widow who gave 2 mites while the rich gave much, that the widow gave the most because she gave not out of her abundance but she gave all that she had, 100% (Mk. 12:42-44). We are never free until we are giving 100% of ourselves so that we are Christ's and he is ours. The great commandment in the law is that we love God with <u>all</u> our hearts, souls and minds (you know you love God when you want to please Him and consequently are obeying Him-Jn. 14:21,23, II Jn. 6) (Mt. 22:36,37).

Jesus plainly tells us that we are entering the kingdom of God when we are **doing** God's will (Mt. 7:21). He tells us that if you believe Jesus is your lord only to the extent that you acknowledge and confess him as "Lord, Lord," you will not be enabled to be entering God's kingdom, the place in which He rules

13

(Mt. 7:21). You have to **participate**. He asks if it is not stupid to call him lord when you are not **doing** (participating in) what he is saying (Lk. 6:46). He tells us that a person who is **doing** the will of his Father in heaven is his "brother and sister and mother" (Mt. 12:50), which makes him a citizen of God's kingdom. He says that his mother and brethren are those who are hearing and **doing** the word of God (Lk. 8:21) and that it is a foolish or <u>stupid</u> man that hears his word, his message, and does not **do** it, does not **participate** (Mt. 7:26,27). You know Jesus if you **do** his commandments (I Jn. 2:3,4). You understand Christianity only if you **do** it. You can know the truth only if you "continue in" **doing** Jesus' "word" (Mt. 8:31,32). Doing your way into right thinking is part of finding truth.

Being irresponsible to **doing** that which we know to be right "is sin" (Ja. 4:17). It is missing the mark and is what causes us to perish. It is <u>stupid</u>. We must overcome <u>stupidity</u> and **do** what is right or we will be destroying ourselves and becoming slaves to our appetites and thus instruments of unrighteousness. We will be perishing (see Jn. 3:16) and not entering God's kingdom, His control.

Jesus said: "blessed are they that hear the word of God and keep [**practice**] it." (Lk. 11:28). He says we are his friends if we **do** whatsoever he commands us, or "is commanding us now" (Jn. 15:14), and we will abide in his love if we are keeping his commandments (daily commandments he gives and his commandments recorded in scripture) the same as he kept God's commandments (Jn. 15:10). He says that he and God will make their dwelling with us if we **keep** or **live by** his words (Jn. 14:23); and he will be making himself known to those who are **doing** his commandments (Jn. 14:21); and that is God's kingdom. We know him only if we are keeping his past and current commandments (I Jn. 2:3,4); and that is the kingdom of God. He is the "author of eternal salvation" **ONLY** "unto all them that obey [**are obeying**] him" (Heb. 5:9), those in his kingdom. We have to **participate** in him; and that is fantastic kingdom **activity**. We need to be fully involved in the **activity** called Christianity. It is liberating, and full of life, opportunity, and challenging adventure.

We can be seeing the kingdom of God only if and when we are "born again" (Jn. 3:3) and we are single minded or "pure in

14

heart" (Mt. 5:8). "EVERY ONE that is born again" is always "like the wind" that you hear but cannot tell where it is going or where it comes from: they are in God's kingdom being **led by God** so that no one knows what God will be **doing** with them or what He has (Jn. 3:8).

To be entering and participating in God's control, the kingdom of God, a person must "be born of the water and of the Spirit" (Jn. 3:5). He must turn from his old self and should, if possible, figuratively bury his old person in <u>water baptism</u> (Rom. 6:4, Col. 2:12); and he must receive the **power to participate** in God's kingdom by being <u>baptized in the Holy Ghost</u> (Lk. 24:49, Acts 1:5,8, Jn. 7:38,39, Jn. 1:33) which is usually accompanied by his speaking in a God-given unknown language. That is not optional.

It is self-evident that when you are in a kingdom you obey the king and labor to know and do his will. Jesus says that his sheep are those individuals who are listening to or hearing his voice and are <u>individually</u> **following** him, **participating** along with him in **doing** <u>what he has them individually do</u> (Jn. 10:27,28) in partnership with him (I Cor. 3:8; II Cor. 6:1; I Pet. 2:5,9; I Cor. 15:58), kingdom partnership. In Jn. 10:28, Jesus says that he is giving his sheep life of the Eternal, what many translations call eternal or everlasting life (literally translated: "age-abiding" or "age-during" life or "life of the Eternal One"). It is kingdom motivation, wisdom, knowledge, passion and ability that Jesus says that you have only as long as you are abiding in him (Jn. 15:1-6); and Jesus defines it as a person's **experientially** knowing him and God (Jn. 17:3). Jesus is giving "eternal life" to his "sheep" (Jn. 10:28). He says that if you are hearing (or remaining steadfast to) his word and "believing on" (being faithful to) God, you have this life of the Eternal God, kingdom life, and will not come into condemnation (Jn. 5:24): and that is salvation pure and simple. You are in Jesus if you are **participating** by keeping his past and daily commandments (I Jn. 3:24; I Jn. 2:3,4,6), being his kingdom. You **do** Christianity.

The Israelites with Moses could have each been priests in God's "kingdom of priests" if they would "be **obeying**" His "**voice**" and keeping His "covenant" (Ex. 19:5,6; Jer. 7:23); **and that without the necessity of Jesus' having come in the flesh.**

15

They would have been "born again," obeying God's voice and living by God's words. But they said: "let not God speak with us" (Ex. 20:19). Jesus' sheep are hearing his voice and obediently **following** him 24/7 (Jn. 10:27): **all** of them are. They are a kingdom of priests (I Pet. 2:5,9, Rev. 1:6,5:10). They will not **follow** a stranger because "they know his [Jesus'] **voice**" and "they know not the voice of strangers" (Jn. 10:4,5). That is God's kingdom.

But many are deaf to his voice (Rev. 3:20) and following the voices of strangers. Hearing his voice is vital and foundational to our being in the kingdom of God and being Jesus' sheep. It is 100% necessary. You "die" to being your own god when you repent: you change to treat God as God.

As with the Israelites with Moses, many people who should be in God's kingdom are saying "let not God speak with us lest we die" (Ex. 20:19). That is going on in the worldly churches. They are following the church programs and selected leaders and listening to mixtures of truth and rubbish. They are not being inconvenienced to be giving up living to themselves (II Cor. 5:15): and they are not living to Jesus (II Cor. 5:15). They are not the kingdom of God.

As men whittle out gods from wooden sticks in pagan cultures, men select the church leaders that please them and call them by religious titles. They make substitutes for Jesus and honor them.

You must die to yourself and die to wanting honor from each other (Jn.5:44, Rom. 2:29; Phil 2:7) if you want to live as a part of God, as His kingdom. Multitudes are saying that they will do what a preacher (man-ordained priest) tells them to do the same as the Israelites said to Moses for him to speak to them and they would hear him instead of directly and individually hearing and **obeying God's "voice"** and their being a "kingdom of priests" (Ex. 19:5,6, Ex. 20:19). Had the Israelites accepted God's offer, there would not have been the law of Moses. Men now are also refusing God's kingdom, refusing hearing God, refusing God. Many pay attractive "leaders" to lie to them and fool them.

You must overcome obeying family, friends, "pastors," and yourself if you want to live to Jesus (Lk. 14:26). You cannot

16

"serve two masters" (Mt. 6:24). Living to Jesus rather than anyone else is a challenge that we MUST win.

Many so-called churches are interested in gaining members and making a name for themselves. They confuse obedience to God with their own ideas of keeping everyone in obedience to them, excited, happy, snookered, involved in activities, believing various doctrines, attracting members by appealing to all kinds of motives, bowing down to leaders, feeling good by supporting building funds, dressing up, pretending love, and much other religious nonsense. They want their victims to obey them rather than themselves fulfilling "The Great Commission" which includes "**teaching them to observe [do] ALL things whatsoever I have commanded you**" (Mt. 28:20). They consider evangelism as getting members but not teaching men to be <u>Jesus' sheep</u> obeying and living to Jesus 24/7.

The whole purpose of the Holy Spirit for us is to give us direct access to God and to give God direct access to us. Wow! And yet many people forfeit participating with God.

Churches point to their successes in obtaining their goals for membership, television appearances, various programs and projects, new and larger buildings, carpet, organs, chandeliers, overhead movie screens, stained glass windows, costumes for their preachers and choirs, public address systems, drums and bands, choirs and such. They are empty of God and are trying to look like the world's churches. Some wear Sunday clothes. They are ignorant they are to be the living holy body of Christ doing only what Jesus is teaching each one to do. Those who do their own things are religiously departing from Christ and choosing a cheap imitation. Those obeying Him know Him.

Many "churches" seek their own glory and want to "make" "a name" for themselves as did the builders of the Tower of Babel (Gen. 11:4). Jesus said "The kingdom of God comes not with observation" (Lk. 17:20) and is "within you" (Lk. 17:21); but they build their kingdoms and gauge themselves by what comes observably through their control, their kingdom. They find it inconvenient to only be God's people. They want the world's admiration.

They do not want the kingdom of God. They are ignorant that they should not have a meeting unless the members are recognizing Jesus and waiting on him for God's fresh ministry through any and all members (I Cor. 14:26-31). They are ignorant that they should be hearing, trusting, and obeying their lord and Shepherd and their Father and caring for one another even to laying down their lives for each other (Jn. 13:34; I Jn. 3:16). They live in delusions.

They are too busy doing their ideas and being proud of themselves for them to be servants ruled by God. There is almost nothing in them that resembles real church. They are like crowds meeting in dark rooms and not knowing there are the light switches of obedience and seeking God and hearing God. They make their own light which is not light. Jesus said: be careful "that the light which is in you be not darkness" (Lk. 11:35). In many cases, people's light is darkness. Men gather to support cherished delusions. They denounce other groups who have different delusions.

It is possible to do wonderful works and prophesy and cast out demons and feel that you are doing the will of God when you are doing iniquity and will be rejected by Jesus (Mt. 7:22,23). A church can believe it is alive when it is dead (Rev. 3:1). It can believe that it is rich spiritually when it is lukewarm, spiritually bankrupt, spiritually blind and naked, and nauseating to Jesus (Rev. 3:16,17).

Satan's job is to deceive (Rev. 12:9, II Cor. 11:14); and he carefully and passionately works at it 24/7. He is successful among many ignorant, gullible, immature, lazy church leaders and followers. They stupidly welcome him.

Jesus himself says: "Few" people "find" the small gate and narrow way "that leads to life" (Mt. 7:14); and, tragically, very few are even looking for it or know their lives depend on their individually finding it for themselves.

Rev. 18:2 speaks of churches that have become "the habitation of devils, and the hold of every foul spirit." God calls His people out of these churches, their churches, in which they are in danger of being participants in the churches' sins (Rev. 18:4). Satan disguises himself as an "angel of light" (II Cor. 11:14) and his ministers are disguised as "ministers of righteousness" (II Cor. 11:14,15), "deceiving and being deceived" (II Tim. 3:13), leading into captivity and going into captivity (Rev. 13:10). They are graduates of seminaries, charismatic leaders, great speakers etc. They are anything but the kingdom of God.

Satan and his ministers are pragmatic: they appear righteous because righteous appearances work with people who are discerning others by their appearances rather than obeying Jesus and knowing authentic Christians by their "fruits" (Mt. 7:16). Satan's deceived ministries are traps for new Christians, "whited sepulchers" (Mt. 23:27).

The kingdom of God is made up of souls that live to God. Jesus "died for all that they which live should not henceforth live unto themselves, but unto him which died for them and rose again" (II Cor. 5:15). He departed from his natural body so he could come back and live IN each participant (Jn. 14:17): "Christ IN you the hope of glory" (Col. 1:27). He did it "for the joy that was set before him" (Heb. 12:2). He needed to become a shepherd (Jn. 10:27,28: I Pet. 2:25) for each and every Christian, the "one [and only] mediator between God and men" (I Tim. 2:5).

"As many as are led by the Spirit of God, they are the sons of God" (Rom. 8:14). "God hath said I will dwell IN them and walk IN them" (II Cor. 6:16). Paul writes to the Philippians: "For it is God which works IN you both to will and to do of His good pleasure" (Phil. 2:13). He says his old self no longer lives, but he lives in faith by the Son of God (Gal. 2:20) and "For me to live is Christ" (Phil. 1:21).

That is the kingdom of God. And God **has no other offer** on the table for any of us. We need not be duped by what men offer even if it is has been popular for 1000 years.

There are lots of substitutes, antichrists, around on every side. Christians must be holy and royal priests (I Pet. 2:5,9), a kingdom of priests (Ex. 19:6, Rev. 1:6, 5:10). They must be inhabited by, in union with, and faithful to Jesus and God. God gives them no other offer. He does not say: "Do what you think is good." He says: "Obey my voice" (Ex. 19:5, Jer. 7:23, Jn. 10:27,28, Lk. 6:46, Rev. 3:20).

Christianity, God's kingdom, does not exist except where men individually make God' kingdom exist by their voluntary individual faithfulness to God, their enthusiastic participation in God and His Son Jesus, their availing themselves of God, their hearing Jesus' voice (Jn. 10:27), trusting God, waiting on and seeking God, and obeying God and Jesus Christ. That is biblical faith: faithfulness, living faith. It is faith that produces works (Ja. 2:14-18) in the great and glorious activity known as Christianity. Abraham is the father or forerunner of "all them that believe" and "the father of US all" (Rom. 4:11,16); and righteousness like his will be considered ours only "if we believe on [are faithful to and trust in] Him [God] that raised up Jesus our Lord from the dead" (Rom. 4:24). Righteousness is living to God as Abraham lived to God and "was called the Friend of God" (Ja. 2:23).

It absolutely requires that we receive the baptism that Jesus would baptize with: the baptism in the Holy Spirit that Jesus said would give us the spiritual "power" that is necessary for us to be able to walk with Jesus (Lk. 24:49, Acts 1:8, Jn. 1:33). And it requires that **we avail ourselves** of the Holy Spirit, Jesus' Spirit, who is sent to (1) cause "rivers of living water" to flow from our bellies (Jn. 7:38,39) and is sent (2) as an "anointing" to teach each of us individually so that we "need not that any man teach" us (we do not need to take a man's word for something) (I Jn. 2:27) and is sent (3) to lead us into all truth (Jn. 16:13) and (4) bring Jesus' sayings to our minds (Jn. 14:26) and (5) to receive from Jesus and give to us (Jn. 16:14). It (6) makes the spiritual person **"judge all things," to be inquiring, seeking, and searching out everything for himself with God helping him and guiding him** (Jn. 16:13) and with the person letting loose of traditional teachings that keep him from God (I Cor. 2:15). The Spirit keeps changing us to be like Jesus (II Cor. 3:18) if we allow Him to do so.

God Himself will, through the Holy Spirit, be a personal tutor to each seeker and will write His laws in his or her individual mind and heart, which is the New Covenant and the kingdom of God (Heb. 8:10). God will do it in His way according to His plan and timing; and that will be different for each person and require his steadfast seeking, obedience and endurance. And each individual will be knowing God and not needing men to be telling him to know God (Heb. 8:11). God gives on-the-job training. We know Him only as we do His will and He comes to live IN us (I Jn. 2:3,4).

Christians are not all alike, they are not all needing the same things, and they do not have the same history or all believe the same way. They must be living to Jesus as their lord and they

20

must be baptized in the Holy Spirit to have power to live to Christ and not to themselves (II Cor. 5:15).

Many human organizations usurp the roles of God, of Jesus and of the Holy Spirit to reveal truth individually to a man. They cut men off from knowing and participating with Jesus and God; and they fool them to believe they do not need the life of the Eternal that they can have by being baptized in God's Spirit and abiding in Christ and participating in the kingdom of God. They make men what they want them to be instead of leaving that job to the Holy Spirit to be "renewing" each person's "mind" (Rom. 12:2) uniquely and differently "from glory to glory" (II Cor. 3:18), layer by layer, the way God wants him to be. God makes snowflakes, fingerprints, DNA and men differently: but men often want men to be and think alike and look like they came off an assembly line that men have programmed.

A church that schedules the time that a meeting will end or the day a "revival" will end, is running off of a different power than the Holy Spirit and should be avoided. God's Spirit does not follow men's plans. The Holy Spirit leads; and the "cart before the horse" will not work. Jesus said "I will build my church" (Mt. 16:18); and Ps. 127:1 says "Except the LORD [Yahweh] build the house, they labor in vain that build it." It is vital that we learn to be "led by the Spirit" and do God's will (Rom. 8:14; Gal. 5:16). A "red flag" should go up in our minds wherever and whenever we find a person or persons who are not waiting on God and following Him and knowing that they are nothing of themselves (I Cor. 3:7). We need to act to protect ourselves from the influence of irresponsible people who continue to act without waiting on Christ and hearing his voice. They appear to know everything and to be full of faith. Anything but obedience to Jesus and being led by the Holy Spirit is just vain labor: "wood, hay, stubble" that is good only to be burned up (I Cor. 3:12,13).

We either choose to individually seek, wait on, listen to, obey, follow and be the vessels of our Lord, or we do our own thing and call it righteousness and salvation. Jesus is the savior only of those who are obeying him (Heb. 5:9). We must repent or give up living to please ourselves and to go along with the crowd that is headed on the path to destruction (Mt. 7:13). Facing and rejecting illusions is difficult and painful. Not facing and rejecting illusions will destroy you while making you feel as good as a man drinking himself into oblivion. Obeying Jesus is salvation.

If you hear God, you need to obey Him. That is wisdom. You are in His hands. He is calling people to a relationship of being His sons and children.

There is a deluded religious world that tells you that God does not expect you to (1) be among the "few there be that find" the "strait [pressed in]" "gate" and "narrow way" "which leads to life" (Mt. 7:14), (2) live to Jesus 24/7 (Jn. 10:27,28, II Cor. 5:15), (3) be pressing into the kingdom of God (Lk. 16:16), (4) be "led by the Spirit of God" (Rom. 8:14) 24/7, (5) "observe all things whatsoever" Jesus "commanded" us (Mt. 28:20), (6) "walk even as he [Jesus] walked" (I Jn. 2:6), (7) be obeying God's voice (Ex. 19:5,6, Jer. 7:23, Lk. 4:4, Rom. 8:14, Rev. 3:20), (8) be "submitting" yourself "one to another in the fear of God" (Eph. 5:23), (9) be a responsible priest of God (I Pet. 2:5,9, Rev. 1:6, 5:10), (10) individually know and live to God as your Father while keeping a good conscience (Mt. 23:9, Rom. 8:15), (11) be taught by the Holy Spirit (I Jn. 2:27, Jn. 16:13), (12) love one another as he loved and loves us (Jn. 13:34, 15:12), (13) live in the New Covenant which is the kingdom of God covenant (Heb. 8:8-12), (14) and be a member of Jesus' active body (or church).

That deluded religious world refuses to take God seriously. They think Christianity is a game instead of its being your very life. They offer and practice an "alternative Christianity," a phony cheap imitation and our enemy. Their leaders do not enter God's kingdom and they keep others out by misdirecting them and giving them a false sense of security (Lk. 11:52). They will be condemned.

If you want God's approval, you need to go out on your own and hold the hand of God and enter into life that is faithful participation with God and Jesus and people who are obeying Jesus and living to him. You want to separate yourself from those who "have a form of godliness, but" deny "the power thereof" (II Tim. 3:5), those who look godly but are not genuinely participating in the powerful essence of God. You need to reject the assurances of religious men and be certain you are hearing God yourself and are being led and taught by Jesus and the Holy Spirit. Men usually set their own rules and live to self-approval. Each of us must make the

22

choice between (1) the shelter of men and organizations that say they know what it is true and right and (2) the shelter of our living directly to Jesus.

The shelter of men with their organizations, hierarchies, beliefs, traditions, practices and irresponsible Bible translations is a veil or curtain between men and God. That veil keeps men from God's life and discourages and forbids that men go directly to God and then hear and obey God.

The greatest and most meaningful experience a man can have is the experience and adventure of living to God each day with God living in him, teaching, leading him, assigning him work (ministry) and changing him from glory to glory. It is the kingdom of God.

3

The Phony Gospel

So what do orthodox churches teach as a substitute gospel for the real gospel, the gospel of the kingdom of God?

Most teach that you are saved if you believe that Jesus is Lord and that he died on the cross for you and he shed his natural blood as a substitutive punishment-bearer for your sins to (1) keep you out of hell and away from his Father's alleged anger and to (2) insure that you will retire to heaven when you die. They teach that you are saved if you are their captive to the extent that (1) you believe and are thankful about what they tell you and (2) you do not dare let the Holy Spirit teach you anything different. When you take the bait this "gospel" offers, you agree that God is mean enough to make people suffer horribly forever. You enter a gospel that is (1) mostly concerned with our being thankful to Jesus for **paying for** our sins and its penalties and (2) is mostly unconcerned with our having any obedient relationship with God, our being God's kingdom.

We will look at it. But what are we being saved from? There is some truth to be said about this that we shall expose later (pp. 47,48: 50: 100,101). But orthodox Christianity says you are being saved from God's anger and from unending torture in hell. And that is likely the most blasphemous, God-hating idea that Satan ever invented. It says that God who "is love" (I Jn. 4:8,16) is going to have many of "His offspring" (Acts 17:29), souls that are His (Ez. 18:4), tortured for no purpose with no remedy forever. It says God is not going to only do away with failures as He once somewhat proposed to Moses (Ex. 32:10) and did to Sodom and Gomorrah (Gen. 31:10) and to Korah and famous men with him (Num. 16:31-33) and did to some extent with a worldwide flood: **it says and subtly requires you participate in believing He is hateful and is going to torture failures forever.**

If you believe that, then you cannot be knowing much about God. Satan says: "Gotcha, I got you misdirected and scared out of your mind with paralyzing ungodly fear that keeps you from sane thinking. You believe God is love and contradictorily that He has a fire in His basement to torture people and make them miserable and hopeless forever. You believe God whose 'hand is not shortened that' He 'cannot save' (Isa. 59:1) and Who is 'not willing that any should perish' (II Pet. 3:9, Ez. 18:32) will fry people forever."

That approaches insanity. It puts the brain out of operation when it teaches it to believe contradictory and blasphemous descriptions of God. It is only tolerated because men are heavily "bewitched" (Gal. 3:1) to believe lies that they have been deceived to accept as truths from God.

One wonders if there are people who subconsciously feel they deserve salvation because they voluntarily give up sanity to believe things that contradict each other.

Men who are paralyzed by fear, choose to ignore not only that (1) "God is love" (I Jn. 4:8,16), but ignore that (2) "God" is "the savior of ALL men" (I Tim. 4:10), that (3) "as in Adam ALL die, even so in Christ shall ALL [the same "ALL"] be made alive [get God's life]" (I Cor. 15:22), that (4) God will one day be "all in all" (I Cor. 15:28), that (5) Jesus is the Mercy Seat (the *King James Version* says "propitiation" and other versions say other things) not only for us but "for the sins of the whole world" (I Jn. 2:2), that (6) God's plan is to "gather together...ALL things in Christ" (Eph. 1:10), that (7) Jesus is to reconcile "ALL things" to God in heaven and in earth (Col. 1:20), that (8) "ALL" of the ancient rebellious Israelites "shall be saved" (Rom. 11:26), that (9) "every knee shall bow" and "every tongue shall confess to God" (Rom. 14:11), that (10) the Savior preached effectively to wicked men who died maybe 5000 years ago before and during the flood (I Pet. 3:19,20), that (11) Sodom with her deceased will yet some day be restored (Ez. 16:55), that (12) there yet will be a "restitution of all things" (Acts. 3:21), that (13) God will "make all things new" (Rev. 21:5), that (14) "all men" will serve the "one like the Son of Man" (Dan. 7:13,14) and that (15) God stated of Himself that He is "merciful and gracious, long suffering, and abundant in goodness and truth...forgiving iniquity, transgression and sin..." (Ex. 34.6,7) and does not change (Mal. 3:6).

The morbid idea that when men die they go to either heaven or hell and remain there unchanged forever is Satan's

26

deadly deceptive invention that is championed by deceived men who hunt souls and bring them into the same destroying delusions ("worms") that they are in. God is not finished with Sodom or with stiff-necked Israelites who departed this world 3500 years ago in the desert. He is not finished with those that died before or in the flood that undoubtedly were changed when Jesus went and preached to them (I Pet. 3:19,20). He is not finished with any of us. All living and deceased people "live unto Him" now (Lk. 21:38). It is evident that where God is there is goodness, life and growth, not stagnation and torture as many believe.

Heb. 9:27 does not say that it "is appointed unto men once to die, but after this *the* judgment;" rather, most all versions and the Greek text differ with the K.J.V. and say "*a* judgment" or "judgment." There is no "the judgment." And Mk. 16:16 does not say that "he that believeth not shall be damned" as the K.J.V. has said; but, it says that a person who refuses to believe shall be condemned. A stubborn person will need correction; and God is expert at giving it.

God has hardly begun the "restitution of all things" (Acts 3:21); and the time will come when He is "all in all" (I Cor. 15:28). Much will change when "The kingdoms of this world [or cosmos] are become the kingdoms of our Lord and of his Christ [his anointed ones]" (Rev. 11:15, Dan. 2:44, Dan. 7:13,14) and the "man child" who will shepherd all nations with an iron rod [not the K.J.V. "rule" all nations] is born (Rev. 12:5) and God "has taken" to Himself His "great power and has reigned" (Rev. 11:17, Dan. 7:9,13,14).

Without violating Jonah's free will, God changed Jonah's heart while he was in a great fish; and He changed arrogant Nebuchadnezzar's heart after making him as a wild animal until "seven times" passed over him (Dan. 4: 32-34). He changed Paul's heart (Acts 9:1-6). God gave Saul "another heart" (I Sam. 10:9). God changes hearts. He Himself hardened the heart of Pharaoh (Ex. 4:21,8:32,10:1) and of Esau (Rom. 9:11-16) and of others (Deut. 2:30, Josh. 11:20, Rom. 9:18). "God" Himself, not people, "concluded [shut up] them ALL [ancient Israelites] in unbelief that He might have mercy upon ALL" (Rom. 11:32): He did not give them just "free will" but "the spirit of slumber, eyes that they should not see and ears that they should not hear" (Rom. 11:8). He

27

can easily bring conditions that will cause the hardest soul to use his own free will to reach out to Him now or in the hereafter. Jesus will lead some departed ones to "living fountains of waters" (Rev. 7:17).

God can and will save all men, living or "dead," as He has said repeatedly (I Tim. 4:10, I Cor. 15:22,28, Col. 1:20, I Jn. 2:2, Eph. 1:10, Rom. 14:11). Hell will be emptied.

The world's churches offer mass religious confusion and carnal incentives; and noble men refuse such nonsense.

Satan is doing his passionate job of deceiving multitudes. He asks you to believe that God is stupid, handicapped, hateful, and a poor planner Who has allowed Satan to wreck His creation and cause untold suffering. Satan has effectively gotten men to believe that God has the characteristics of Satan and also that he, Satan, is out of God's control and has power that is independent of God.

So, Satan, having gotten his slander of God into man's Bible translations and into men's minds, invents a totally false solution to the false situation which he invented and in which he says men find themselves with this god he describes as being vindictive, mean, weak, without foresight, uncaring, irresponsible and not worthy of trust.

Satan used Archbishop Anselm of Canterbury in A.D. 1098 to argue against the 900-year-old orthodox dumb idea that Jesus' crucifixion was God's appropriate compensation to Satan for His taking men back from Satan. Anselm disagreed with the old rubbish and invented his own rubbish: that God was like the lord of a medieval manor who had been offended by a lowly serf that lived in his domain and was due whatever satisfaction this lord of the manor might require of the serf. He invented the "satisfaction" theory that is the foundation of modern orthodox teaching that says that Jesus died for our sins as a substitute for us and as a way of getting a disgruntled, disappointed, offended god satisfied with sinful men. It says that Jesus' death and shed blood satisfied God so that we did not have to take God's wrath and punishment.

Rom. 3:24,25 in the *New Living Translation* of the Bible says that God rescued men from His anger and from paying penalties for their sins by having Jesus be a sacrifice, and that when people believe that Jesus was a sacrifice for men and shed his blood they are reconciled to God. *The Living Bible* says Jesus came to be punished in our place and to remove God's anger at men. These are Anselm's teaching from A.D. 1098; and they are the basis of orthodox theology today. Both this substitutive theory and the earlier theory taught by Irenaeus and Origen around A.D. 200 are stupid and teach non-participation in God while they claim to give revelation of God. Jesus said: "they that worship Him [God] must worship Him in spirit and in truth" (Jn. 4:24), not in evil imaginations.

Traditional teachings of (1) God being offended and needing a substitute to satisfy His alleged ill will and (2) of God's giving Jesus' death to reimburse Satan for His taking men from him, are powerful and destructive. They turn men over to useless activity and frustration; and multitudes prefer these deceptions to reality and truth. Each of these teachings was or is now reverenced as being God's message to men. They are ridiculous unscriptural gospels that destroy men.

The teachings of Jesus' taking our punishment in place of us, the teaching that God burns men in hell forever, and the teaching that wicked men will not be saved after their deaths are all lies that will prevent men from knowing God and trusting a god who let Satan destroy his creation and has no plan to save all his people, but one to torture many.

Ideas of never-ending suffering after death are not at all in the Old Testament. The only "hell" of the Old Testament is the wrongly translated Hebrew *Sheol* meaning the place of the righteous and wicked departed souls or the "unseen state." It is equal to the Greek *Hades* of the New Testament that is also rendered incorrectly as *hell* in the K.J.V. Both *Sheol* and *Hades* are incorrectly rendered "hell" in the K.J.V.; and that is the cause and support of a lot of false teachings, confusion and misdirected men.

The rich man that had no compassion for the beggar Lazarus did not go to hell in Jesus' story (Lk. 16:19-31). Rather, he went to *Hades,* the place of the dead, which included Paradise, to which Lazarus also went. He did suffer, but he is not said to have gone to hell in Jesus' story as the K.J.V. says he did. As the *New King James Version* and many other translations say, the rich man

29

went to *Hades*, which is not characteristically a place of correction or suffering.

If Jesus is not actively your Lord that you are obeying and living to, you are not saved regardless of what you believe in your mind about him or his death on the cross and his shed natural blood and regardless of what supernatural experiences you have had. Jesus himself said that you will be "cast forth" from him and "withered" if you do not "abide" (or participate) in him (Jn. 15:6) and that he is nauseated by lukewarm Christians and will vomit them out of himself (Rev. 3:16,17) and that a servant of his that knows but does not do his will shall be cast into outer darkness and weep and gnash his teeth (Mt. 25:26-30). Heb. 5:9 says Jesus is the "author of eternal salvation unto all them that obey [are obeying] him." **The kingdom gospel of participation in God is true; and orthodox gospel is phony!** The orthodox is wickedly misdirecting.

Correctly translated, Jn. 3:16 does not say that you have everlasting or Eternal life if you believe in Jesus. It says that you have Eternal life if you are continually obeying, trusting in, and being faithful to (Greek *pistueon eis*) Jesus. Just believing in Jesus will just get you delusion. When Jn. 3:16 is wrongly translated, as it usually and popularly is, it causes the spiritual downfall of numerous "Christians." Remember: "the devils also believe, and tremble;" and just believing or "faith without works is dead" (Ja. 2:20,24).

You have the life of the Eternal, Eternal life, if you continuously trust in and depend on and live in obedience to the Eternal God and His son Jesus. Your faith must be faithfulness, trust, and obedience. Your mental belief (1) that Jesus is God's son or (2) is Lord or (3) that Jesus died for your sins will not save you or give you Eternal life. You must "abide in" Jesus, **be participating in him** (Jn. 15:6).

Eternal life does not describe unending life of the soul. It describes the divine kind of life. Jesus defines it as one's having an experiential knowledge of "the only true God and Jesus Christ" (Jn. 17.3). He says emphatically that you have this life if you are listening to his word and being faithful to God (Jn. 5:24). You do not have it if you are not listening to Jesus and being faithful to God. It is God's life; and Jesus says it is available, but only if and when we abide (participate) in Jesus (Jn. 15:1-6).

30

You abide in Jesus if you are hearing his voice and following his leading (Jn. 10:27,28) and are keeping (doing) his commandments (I Jn. 3:24) and he is your active lord (Lk. 6:46). A person who says he <u>knows</u> Jesus and is not keeping "his commandments is a liar and the truth is not in him" (I Jn. 2:4). And if he does not <u>know</u> Jesus, he does not have eternal life (Jn. 17:3).

Being saved is participating in Christianity, obeying Jesus (Heb. 5:9). Salvation comes to a person when he or she is born from above by the will of God (Jn. 1:13) to REPENT (Mt. 4:17, Acts 2:38, Mk. 2:17) and be repenting, which is for him or her to be changing his or her understandings and activities to serve and live to Jesus and God. It may or may not involve a singular supernatural experience that impresses a person greatly, although many erroneously believe that a singular life-changing experience is all there is to being saved and "born again." It will involve a multitude of experiences where a person often does not even recognize God's hand. But however it is that God deals with a person, salvation includes a person's being changed from "glory to glory" until he is fully like Jesus (II Cor. 3:18). He must "work out" his "own salvation" (Phil. 2:12) or lose it. He himself must overcome ungodliness (Rev. 3:21) and "rule over" "sin" (Gen. 4:7).

Many people believe that eternal life is just unending life; but they believe that people in hell have unending life also.

The life of God is unending, but a man can easily lose that "eternal" life and walk away from it by not carefully and faithfully living to God and Jesus. Eternal life is a kind of life. You must stay plugged into Christ (Jn. 15:1-6) and be participating in him if you are to have God's Life. You are "saved" only if you are presently obeying Jesus (Heb. 5:9).

"Work on the cross" beliefs are offspring of the ideas that Jesus took our punishment for sin and did away with God's imagined anger toward men (see pages 28,29). These false "work on the cross" beliefs are contradictory to the scriptures and they blind men to the truths: that (1) Jesus was crucified and rejected the same way James and John would soon be treated when they would "drink indeed of" Jesus' cup and be "baptized with the baptism that" Jesus was "baptized with" (Mt. 20:23), that (2) we are commanded to have "this mind" "in" us, "which was also in

31

Christ" who "humbled himself and became obedient unto death, even the death of the cross" (Phil. 2:5,8), that (3) "Christ also suffered for us, leaving us an EXAMPLE that" we ourselves "should follow his steps [not just thank and praise him for what he did, but do what he did]" (I Pet. 2:21), that (4) we are to "arm" ourselves "likewise with the same mind" as "Christ" who "suffered for us in the flesh" (I Pet. 4:1), and that (5) Jesus did not get God to change for us: Jesus was living with God IN him as Emmanuel, "God with us:" his actions were God's (Jn. 5:19, 12:49, 14:10).

The phrase saying "by whose stripes ye were healed" of I Pet. 2:24 refers not to physical healing but to the next verse: "but [you] are now returned unto the Shepherd and Bishop of your souls" (I Pet. 2:25), a spiritual healing.

There are more beliefs about a "work on the cross" giving us benefits. They are phony, misdirecting imaginations, or delusions that Jesus earned "virtue" we can use as benefits. And that is much easier than and is the opposite from your asking God, believing God and waiting on and trusting Him, as Jesus and the apostles teach us to do (Mt. 7:7, Mt. 7:11, Ja. 5:15, Phil. 4:6, Ja.4:2, Mt. 18:19, Mt. 21:22).

Peter's saying "Who his own self bare our sins in his body on the tree" likely refers to men having hated God and killed Jesus which Jesus expressed in Jn. 15:23,24 and Peter and Paul spoke of many times later in Acts, which brought men to repentance (Acts 2:36,37, 3:15, 4:10, 5:30, 7:52, 10:39, 13:27-29 etc).

Theologians and translators are well entrenched in beliefs that have been passed down for centuries. Men follow and fear to not trust them. These beliefs are polluted spiritual waters that make men sick and kill them spiritually.

Translators copy each other and sell books. Since John Wycliffe in the 14th century, they have translated the Bible to tell the substitution ideas of Anselm and ideas of men ruling men. We are trying to untangle more of the wrong beliefs, the "worms" and "viruses" as computer people would call them, which are preventing God's kingdom.

First, is orthodox teaching right? Did Jesus' shed blood and death on the cross bring about the forgiveness of sins?

Ex. 34:6,7, Ps. 103:3, II Chr. 7:14, Ez. 18:21,22, Mic. 7:18, Isa. 55:7, and Jn. 5:24 are scriptures we should memorize that guarantee that **God's nature and practice is and has always been to forgive sins** and that God had no problem forgiving sins. He definitely did not require nor need that Jesus die to enable Him to "forgive" sins. So why will we disbelieve God, become misdirected and believe that God could not forgive sins without Jesus' death or shed natural blood? We are then making up a nonexistent problem and then making up a solution so that we can ignore the truths of what Jesus did as an **example** and what his followers must be ready to do. Ignoring his example is refusing him. **If you do not see that you are to live as Jesus did (I Jn. 2:6), "overcome" as he "overcame" (Rev. 3:21), follow his <u>example</u> of suffering (I Pet. 2:21), and be made perfect (mature) and learn obedience through suffering (Heb. 5:8; 2:10), you will be ignorant of and likely oppose what Christ is doing in you and in other Christians.**

God never needed Jesus to die or shed blood so He could "forgive" sins. He had been "forgiving" sins for thousands of years before Jesus came to earth and He does not change (Mal. 3:6). Jesus forgave sins before his death (Mt. 9:2-6. Lk. 7:48) and John's baptism was a baptism of repentance expressly for the forgiveness of sins (Lk. 3:3). How stupid, misdirected and blasphemous it is to think God needed Jesus' death so He could forgive sins! Men have become thankful to Jesus for what was not needed or done and have become ignorant of what he did. **The center of many peoples' worship is a deception that keeps them from authentic righteousness, ongoing salvation, God and the gospel of the kingdom that Jesus preached. They thank God wrongly and fail to obediently participate in God.**

It was always repentance, a change in one's soul, heart, actions and thinking that was necessary to rid men of sin and secure "forgiveness." Only repentance, an authentic change in you, satisfies you and God concerning your sins (II Chr. 7:14, Isa. 55:7, Ez. 18:21,22), though it does not eliminate civil or criminal penalties for sins. Rebellious men choose to believe they do not need repentance, being changed in their hearts, activities, actions, goals, and beliefs.

Orthodox doctrine says it was God who needed to be changed. It boggles the mind to know that people think it was God that needed changing rather than that it is them.

God does not enjoy punishing people. He has "no pleasure in the death of the wicked" (Ez. 18:23). Repentance, change in the spiritual heart, makes a person a different person, one who is no longer guilty. He, under God's influence, has judged his old self and put him under the judgment of death, which in biblical language is "the shedding of blood" (Gen. 9:6, Gen. 37:22, Heb. 9:22). The offender, the man's wicked old self, has been judged and killed by repentance and is dead. Jesus and John the Baptist told the people to repent so they could be in the kingdom of God and be the kingdom of God (Mt. 3:2, 4:17).

Repentance is a much bigger thing than most people realize. It is not saying that you are sorry. It is not asking for forgiveness. For one man it meant that he had to "sell whatsoever" he "had and give to the poor" and "take up the cross" and "follow" Jesus (Mk. 10:21). For anyone it means that holding a wife or child or other family member or one's own life or soul as more dear than Jesus will make it impossible to be a disciple (Lk. 14:26). Not persevering in carrying your cross and following Jesus or not forsaking all you have, will make it impossible to be Jesus' disciple (Lk. 14:27,33). Repenting consists of your changing your thinking, your activities, your friends and all of you to be a vessel inhabited by Jesus. It does not happen all at once. We continually press into God's kingdom (Lk. 16:16). It requires drastic changes. You grow from glory to glory. It is inspired and led by Jesus, the Shepherd; and it must be done so that you can live to and obey Jesus. It requires trusting and hearing God and requires your motives changing from selfishness to God-supplied love.

And yet the ungodly, ignorant orthodox belief is that Jesus' shed blood is to be trusted as having satisfied God. And that gives birth to shameless, ignorant, delusional, false Christianity.

That idea effectively keeps people from knowing God, blasphemes God, and gives them **delusional salvation**.

You get your sins "forgiven" or taken away when **you change**, you repent so as to have a changed mind and heart that makes you a new person, a "new creature" (II Cor. 5:17, Gal. 6:15). Being "born again" was not something introduced by Jesus; it had been available and understood long before Jesus taught it to Nicodemus. In fact, Jesus asked Nicodemus how he could be "a master" (teacher) of Israel and not know "these things" (Jn. 3:10).

You could be "born again" and get forgiveness of sins before Jesus was killed. Enoch, Abraham, Moses and others were "born again" and "led by the Spirit" and were righteous (Gen. 15:6, Heb. 11:5, Gen. 15:6, Rom. 4:9,11,16,23-24).

Multitudes of Christians, pagans, and Anselm have stupidly assumed that God is offended and needs satisfying.

Translators have spoken a lot about God "forgiving" sins; and it is logical to believe that God has been offended if He forgives sins. The New Testament Greek words that have to do with His forgiving are *aphiemi* which literally means to "send away," *charizomai* that means to "bestow favor unconditionally," and *apolou* that means to "let loose" or "release." None of them indicates that anyone has been offended or is forgiving people. Sending sin away, bestowing favor, and letting loose of sins do not require that anyone be offended or forgive sins. Likewise, the Old Testament rightly translated words for "forgive" do not indicate that someone has been offended. God, who is love, would be much less than God if He were ever offended. It would be like a father being offended with his two-year-old son. God does not "forgive sins." He changes sinners.

But now let us recognize that the problem was not that God was handicapped and could not or would not forgive (send away) sins because He was offended. As we said on pages 28,29, Archbishop Anselm and Satan invented that idea in A.D. 1098. Anselm decided that God was like the lord of a medieval manor who was due "satisfaction" if one of his serfs (common working men) offended him; and he decided that men had offended God by their sins. To pretend to psychoanalyze God and declare God to be like a lord of a manor is blasphemous and stupid and is a violation of God's commandment that we are not to make any graven image "or any likeness of any thing that is in heaven above" (Ex. 20:4). However, Anselm thought his theory was better than the theory that had been in vogue for the previous 900 years that said God was giving Jesus' death to Satan in return for God's taking men away from him. Anselm said that Satan did not deserve anything from God because he got man by deception. Foolish people make up such teachings and millions of foolish or fooled people follow and add to them and are followed by other fooled people for hundreds of years. It is mind boggling.

Anselm's theory is a type of what was believed by ungodly tribes and pagans all over the planet who sacrificed animals and humans to influence their imaginary gods and make the imaginary gods favorably disposed toward them. It was a thought that God had a bad temper and anger toward men that could be calmed by a sacrifice that would propitiate Him, would make Him propitious or well disposed toward men. Men had had this concept for thousands of years. They did not know, as many Christians still do not know, that it is themselves that need to change.

Aristotle, to the contrary, had said that God is the Unmoved Mover, One who is above being controlled by men or their actions. The Hebrew people stood alone as a people having the sane understanding similar to Aristotle's that they could not persuade or manipulate God to do their desires. God propitiates men: no one can propitiate God; and God does not need to be propitiated. "God was in Christ reconciling [propitiating] the world unto Himself" (II Cor. 5:19), not reconciling Himself to men. God is not manipulated or propitiated. He does not change (Mal. 3:6).

The idea that God is ever angry is one that makes Him less than God. The Bible uses **anthropomorphic** terms about God's eyes, hands, right arm, mouth, fierce anger, wrath etc. But God is God. He knows all that will happen before it happens (Acts 15:18, Rom. 4:17) and He has ability to shape things and to change things as He wishes. He gives full attention to billions of people at the same time. Men's anger arises from frustration, surprise happenings and difficulties. God has none of these to contend with. He "works all things after the counsel of His own will" (Eph. 1:11); and "He does according to His will in the army of heaven and among the inhabitants of the earth, and none can stay His hand..." (Dan. 4:35). He planned for Jesus' and our ministries "before the foundation of the world" (Rev. 13:8, Rom. 8:29, Mt. 25:34, Eph. 1:4-6, Heb. 4:3).

The thought that God can be propitiated is nowhere in scripture. Sacrifices were reminders of sin under the law (Heb. 10:3) and could not "take away sins" (Heb. 10:4,11). We must be propitiated or made favorably disposed toward God, reconciled to God. As the II Cor. 5:19 manuscript tells us that "God was [**and is**, Gk. imperfect] in Christ reconciling the world unto Himself ...," II

Cor. 5:20 tells **us**, not Jesus, to do our part and "be ye reconciled to God." Obviously, **we** have to be making an effort to be reconciled to God **now**. That was not done for us by a substitute.

In Rom. 3:25, Jesus was not, as the K.J.V. has it, "set forth to be a propitiation through faith in his blood" but is our "mercy seat" (Ex. 25:22) set forth in his soul or life ("blood" is often biblical language for "soul" or "life"-see pages 38 and 42) we access through faith, trust and faithfulness. Major translations differ widely at Rom. 3:25.

Jesus said he did not come to be an Old Testament type sacrifice "offered by the law" but that he **replaced** those sacrifices by doing God's will (Heb. 10:8,9, Ps. 51:16,17).

It is darkness and stupidity for men to try to change God: it repudiates the truth that it is man, not God, who needs to be changed. It causes us to miss that the problem is men's out-of-control carnal nature. It causes men to look for an answer to the nonexistent problem that God needs to be changed, though God does not change. And it teaches men to not follow Jesus' **example** but to praise him for doing what their carnal natures do not want to do. It teaches that men are put into harmony with God not by their being changed but by a substitute. It refutes Christianity.

The real salvation is that we get changed to be in union with God, serving God in God's kingdom as Jesus did.

God has always loved His creation that He is creating and not needed to be reconciled to it. God knows every act of every man and he knows men's needs before they pray concerning them (Mt. 6:8). He knows the ignorance, darkness and blindness of heart that they have, by His will, when they are born into in this world "shaped in iniquity" (Ps. 51:5). He said before the flood "that every imagination of the thoughts of" man's "heart was only evil continually" (Gen. 6:5); and after the flood He said "for the imagination of man's heart is evil from his youth" (Gen. 8:21).

Men are "shaped in iniquity" and conceived in sin (Ps. 51:5) and "ALL have sinned and come short of the glory of God" (Rom. 3:23). Without Christ, "there is none righteous" (Rom. 3:10). God numbers the hairs on men's heads (Mt. 10:30). He also knows that men are born into an evil world without experience or His Spirit ruling in them and are consequently incapable of doing things right. God wants it that way so men will seek Him so they can be right and do right when they discover that they need good and need to hate iniquity. He wants them to have "their **senses exercised** to discern both good and evil" "<u>by reason</u> **of use**" (Heb. 5:14). It is judging good and bad, making decisions, learning, and **experience**. Men change their souls, make new circuits in their minds, and give God access to their heart as they "work out their salvation" (Phil. 2:12).

God does not change because of a sacrifice; but He declares "For I am the LORD [Yahweh], I change not ["I don't have moods. I am not swayed to do men's will"]" (Mal. 3:6). Ja. 1:17 says that in God "there is no variableness, neither shadow of turning."

To understand what the blood of Jesus does, you must first understand what it is. It is metaphorically the soul or life (Greek *psuche,* Hebrew *nephesh*) of Jesus. God told Noah: "But the flesh with the life [or "soul"] thereof, which is the blood thereof, shall you not eat" (Gen. 9:4). God told Moses that "the life [or "soul"] of the flesh is in the blood" (Lev. 17:11) and that the blood "is the life [or "soul"] of all flesh" and "the life [or "soul"] of all flesh is the blood thereof" (Lev. 17:14). Paul, telling people who knew he had not knifed anyone, said he had not taken advantage of or damaged anyone: "I am pure from the <u>blood</u> [souls] of all men" (Acts 20:26). Jesus corrected some of his followers' thinking by telling them he was not referring to his natural blood as the agent that gave them his life. He had been talking metaphorically about eating his flesh and drinking his blood (blood is flesh also). He said the Spirit gives life, and that the flesh, his natural body and blood, are not of any value to be eaten and drunk: "the flesh profits nothing" (Jn. 6:63). They are spiritually worthless; and it is idolatry to think you should drink a representation of Jesus' natural blood rather than a representation of his life or soul.

You must be drinking the blood of Jesus or (1) you have no life in you and (2) you are not dwelling in him and having him dwelling in you (Jn. 6:53-56). You must take in Jesus' soul or life if you want eternal life. "Christ IN you" is your "hope of glory" (Col. 1:27). Jesus' people are each members of Jesus' living body, parts of Jesus and parts of each other having Jesus' soul or life in them and directing them (Rom. 12:5, Eph, 4:25, I Cor. 6:15, I Cor. 12:12,27).

Jesus said it was good for him to die so he could send the Holy Spirit (Jn. 16:7) that would come in his name (Jn.14:26; 7:37-39) and join him into a personal one-on-one relationship and union (Jn. 14:18,19) with all who were baptized not in physical water but in the Holy Ghost "living water" (Jn. 4:10,14, Jn. 7:37-39, Acts 1:5,8. Lk. 24:49) and who then availed themselves of him. Jesus now is unlimited and has God's abilities (Col. 2:9) so that he can live in and give full attention to each of billions of men and women in what to us is all at the same time! That is the kingdom of God that is making us the kingdom of God, God's realm.

But to be saved, you must die. Jesus did not have to die as a substitute for your sins: you must die to your sinful nature and be "born again" to a new spiritual life and become a "new creature" or "new creation" (II Cor. 5:17, Gal. 6:15). You must give up living to yourself and your ideas; and you must orient yourself to live to God (II Cor. 5:15). That is repentance. You must be denying yourself (saying "no" to yourself-Mt. 16:24) and be about the activities God has for you. "For he that is dead is freed [literally: "made righteous"] from sin" (Rom. 6:7). There is no other way.

Water baptism is a voluntary premeditated burial service (Rom. 6:4; Col. 2:12) in which you bury your old self by deserting who you have been; and then you look to Jesus with "a good conscience toward God" (I Pet. 3:21) and participate in Christ. You reorient yourself to live to Jesus.

Being "born again" is not just a death to who you were. It is not getting "all dressed up with nowhere to go" as would be the case if you only had your past sins "forgiven." Rather it is participation in Christ so that you are being led by God so no one knows where you are going or where you came from, "so is EVERY ONE THAT IS BORN OF THE SPIRIT" (Jn. 3:8). God comes into you, makes you a "new creature," and employees you with on-the-job training.

You do not get rid of sin by believing Jesus was your substitute. That belief will cause you to keep sin, your sinful nature, and enter deception. It would be like believing you were healed from cancer because an unqualified person said so. It will frustrate you to think Jesus' death took away your sin, because you will not have had anything actually done about your sinful heart that is "deceitful above all things and desperately wicked" (Jer. 17:9) and is in need of a savior and shepherd, a new life, and metamorphosis. Your former habits of watching sports religiously, neglecting family, cheating and lying, having bad friends, giving way to a bad temper etc. are things you give up so you can participate in God. And it takes Christ in you giving you eternal life, his life, for you to live in him and above sin. "Walk in the Spirit and you shall not fulfill the lust of the flesh" (Gal. 5:16). Do not walk in the Spirit and it is guaranteed you will be led by your carnal nature and be "carnally minded" which is "death" (Rom. 8:6) and "enmity against God" (Rom. 8:7). Few walk in the Spirit.

God had (1) directly forbidden substitutive satisfaction of sins and (2) had said additionally that "every man shall be put to death for his own sin" (Deut. 24:16, II Chr. 25:4, Jer. 31:30). Anselm's substitution belief is unscriptural and rebellion to God. It is deception and keeps men from finding salvation through dying to themselves and living to God. You pay for sins, if you want to call it that, by dying to the person you were. You die to your sinful, independent nature that you, by God's will, were born into: and you live by Christ in you when you are "born again." **You get born again from above and become a "new creature" or "new creation" (II Cor. 5:17, Gal. 6:15). You repent or get changed in your thinking and actions: and you start on the road from where you are to where you are being "changed…from glory to glory" (II Cor. 3:18) being "not conformed to this world" but being "transformed by the renewing of your mind" (Rom. 12:2), not by the phony substitution gospel.**

You find out that when you sin you are destroying yourself. It is not about your allegedly disappointing God or causing Him anger: it is about your destroying yourself from knowing God and participating in Him and having integrity before Him. Of course, God will intervene at some point in this life or the hereafter if you continue to be <u>stupid</u> and make bad decisions and destroy yourself; and that will not necessarily be pleasant. You can destroy yourself from your being in God's kingdom, His living in you. God gives us the opportunity to escape carnality and live spiritually knowing Him. That is our future. God will bring it to pass. He will be "all in all." Men and women will smarten up.

You should go from being not glorious to being a vessel of God and a part of Jesus and God. You learn to live and think the same way Jesus lived and thought (I Jn. 2:6); and the Holy Spirit makes you successful if you do not give up (Phil. 1:6, Ro. 8:28,37). By God's plan, you are coming from spiritual depravity into perfection; and God comes in the Holy Spirit and Jesus to work in you to make you what you need to be (II Cor. 3:18, Phil. 1:6, Phil. 2:13) and to be there to help you if you sin and repent and confess your sins (I Jn. 1:9,2:1). "He that does righteousness is righteous" (I Jn. 3:7): he does the ways of God's kingdom.

So be smart and do not believe that Jesus did everything for you. Others may avoid what God has said. You must die to your old self and overcome the things that are out of control in your life and keeping you from God's direction and right ways. Jesus said: "To him that overcomes will I grant to sit with me in my throne, even as I overcame and am set down with my Father in His throne" (Rev. 3:21). We do as Jesus did. God told Cain <u>he</u> must overcome sin (Gen. 4:7).

Notice that sins are acts of sin. They are the product of sin which is the unregenerate, dishonest, selfish, stupid, spiritually dead, malformed, ignorant heart and mind prodded by the deceiving devil and by one's own fleshly desires and injured soul. Jesus changes hearts and minds to not commit acts of sin: he gets rid of and replaces the sin in us that produces sins. He deals with causes of sins.

Altar calls are products of guilt that people will have if they have been misguided to believe that what Jesus did on the cross changed them such that repentance and living by a new life, kingdom life, is not what sets them free and keeps them from "a conscience of sins" (Heb 10:2). I Jn. 3:6 tells us that (only) "whosoever abides in him sins not," the emphasis being on abiding in him which we do if we are keeping his commandments (I Jn. 3:24). Only "Whosoever is born of God sins not [does not keep on sinning]" (I Jn. 5:18). Altar calls are for (1) those who do not have the power to "walk in the Spirit" (Gal. 5:16) because they are not baptized in the Holy Spirit and they are for (2) those who are baptized in the Spirit but are not living in the Spirit and for (3) those who listen to and believe Satan who, with his many human

41

helpers, is "the accuser of our brethren" and deceiver of the "whole world" (Rev. 12:9,10).

And notice also that sin is not always rebellion against God. It means a missing of the target. It is error, failure or rebellion. It is often mistranslated. Paul, who said he had been "chief" among sinners (I Tim. 1:15), obtained mercy for persecuting Christians unto death because he did it "ignorantly" (I Tim. 1:13). Many religious people and groups commit sin (error) by their vain worship that is not "in spirit and in truth" (Jn. 4:23,24). The "spirit" and the "truth" are little practiced and known: however, Jesus said that "they which worship Him [God] **MUST** worship Him in spirit and in truth" (Jn. 4:24). Neglecting truth is error and sin, a substitute for true worship and for the strait gate and narrow way that lead to life (Mt. 7:14). Neglect of truth can send "Christians" to hell (Lk. 13:24-28, II Thes. 2:10).

The blood of Jesus, as we have said before, is the soul or life of Jesus. It is Jesus. And only that blood, Jesus in you, can do away with sin in you. It happens now and in you, not 2000 years ago in Israel in someone else. You must be actively in union with Jesus or you will be in union with the desires of your flesh and mind (Gal. 5:16) that do not obey God (Rom. 8:7). They will treacherously trick you (Jer. 17:9) and prevent your being in God's control and family.

"The blood of Jesus" will "cleanse us from all sin" (I Jn. 1:7): Jesus will "cleanse us from all unrighteousness" (I Jn. 1:9). Jesus and the blood of Jesus are the same.

It is not the shed natural blood that helps us overcome sin. It is the living blood, Jesus in us actively guiding and influencing, leading and speaking, carrying us through metamorphosis, and willing and doing God's will in us (Phil. 2:13) that keeps us from sin. "Whosoever is born of God does not [continue to] commit sin, for His seed [divine life] remains in him, and he cannot sin [be sinning] because he is born of God" (I Jn. 3:9), he is participating in God, dwelling in the Vine, living as part of God's kingdom under the New Covenant.

We need to grow up and quit making childish explanations. We need to deal with spiritual reality and refuse any voice but Jesus' and any solution but that that is real. Those Christians who do not love the truth enough to obey God and live

42

by it and **suffer for it** will be sent strong delusion by God so they can be judged for not loving the truth and for consequently doing evil (II Thes. 2:11,12). They are walking the wide, easy path to destruction (Mt. 7:13). For them to see their stupidity for what it is and then be brought to repentance, their sin must be shown to them by God. God has sympathy and remedies for those trapped in delusions of their own making and of respected men.

We have a carnal nature, a mind that was educated and taught by our natural body and mind with a purpose of survival, pleasure and comfort. We call him our "old man" (Eph. 4:22, Col. 3:9), the person or self we were before we were joined to God through Jesus and buried our "old man" in water baptism. We bury him in baptism but we must keep our flesh from resurrecting him and using the old memory circuits in our brains that were useful for ungodliness. We choose our way to heaven, the kingdom of God, godliness. We choose God or carnality (Rom. 8:6).

Our minds must be being renewed and transformed (Rom. 12:2). My "old man," though he is dead as long as I keep him dead by denying myself (my old man), is at war with my spiritual nature and mind that are alive and undergoing metamorphosis or transformation by Jesus through the Holy Spirit and are in union with Jesus (Phil. 1:6, II Cor. 3:18, Rom. 12:2). We often consult our "old man" before rejecting his flawed wisdom and overcoming his advice. He and others offer convenience, pleasure, comfort, lies, quick and easy solutions, and spiritual death.

We are handicapped by that old self although he has been put out of commission by our rejecting, abandoning, and burying him and by our hearts being turned to be serving God. He is kept out of commission by our living to Jesus "in newness of life" (Rom, 6:4) and not to ourselves (II Cor. 5:15). **If** we "walk in the Spirit," we "will not fulfill the lusts of the flesh" (Gal. 5:16). The cure for sin is Christ in us and our choosing Jesus instead of the temptations he is helping us overcome as long as we do not give up. The blood of Jesus, Jesus, takes away sin. Jesus brings us to repentance which alone frees us from sin (Mt. 9:13).

We have to "know to refuse the evil and choose the good" as Jesus did (Isa. 7:15). We must have our **"senses exercised** to discern both good and evil" "by reason of use," by <u>experience</u> (Heb. 5:14). And there is absolutely no other way we can understand good and evil except that the Holy Spirit carry us through a lot of <u>experiences</u> that at first seem unreasonable. We will quickly discover that we know almost nothing about good and evil until we experience being made "perfect through sufferings" (Heb. 2:10).

We are not fully godly at all, but we are undergoing transformation or metamorphosis to be a totally new type of creature. We will "bear the image of the heavenly" Adam Jesus (I Cor. 15:49); we will have been changed "from glory to glory" into Jesus' image or likeness by the Spirit (II Cor. 3:18). Our minds are being transformed (going through metamorphosis-Rom. 12:2; II Cor. 3:18); and we will "be conformed to the image of His [God's] son" Jesus, "the firstborn among many brethren" (Rom. 8:29), and be "joint-heirs with Christ if so be that we suffer with him" (Rom. 8:17).

Suffering weans us off of our dependence on pleasures and causes us to be depending on and fulfilled by God. Paul was "pressed out of measure, above strength, insomuch that" he "despaired even of life" so he "should not trust in" himself "but in God..." (II Cor. 1:8,9). God teaches us a lot through suffering we find ourselves in when we are in God. Multitudes choose easy ways and do not "suffer with him" and consequently will not soon be "joint-heirs" with Christ (Rom. 8:17). "For our light affliction, which is but for a moment, works FOR US a far more exceeding and eternal weight of glory" (II Cor. 4:17).

We do not have to obey our "old man." We learn to reject and overcome him and get a rebuilt mind through Christ who is alive in us. Our new persons, ourselves as "new creations" (II Cor. 5:17, Gal. 6:15), desire to keep in union and participation with Jesus and God Who are life to us.

Paul warned the Ephesian Christians to not live as other Gentiles live, "in the vanity of their mind, having the understanding darkened, being alienated from the life of God through the ignorance that is in them, because of the blindness of their heart, who being past feeling have given themselves over to lasciviousness to work all uncleanness with greediness" (Eph. 4:17-19). All that "backsliding" is probable for those who do not live daily and closely to the Shepherd of their souls. It is happening to "Christians."

44

We need to say something about the *King James Version* translation of II Cor. 5:21. It states that God made Jesus "to be sin for us, who knew no sin; that we might be made the righteousness of God in him." *Sin* was the Old Testament term for the sin sacrifice. William Tyndale, who was the first to translate the New Testament into English from the Greek New Testament, wrote in A.D. 1534 beside II Cor. 5:21: "sin is an offering for sin, as afore. Rom. 8." At Rom. 8, he has: "sin is taken here for a sin-offering after the use of the Hebrew tongue." The K.J.V. rendering seems far less than honest and their translators seem to this writer to be discredited by their omission of any reference to the content of Tyndale's 2 notes, even though they were forbidden to insert notes. The K.J.V. New Testament is over 75% a copy of Tyndale's translation, so its translators were quite familiar with his notes and did not use them or acknowledge their content at this crucial rendering. The Rotherham Bible, the *Concordant Literal New Testament,* the Charles B. Williams New Testament, the *New International Version*, the *New English Bible*, Tyndale's "Plowboy" New Testament translated in 1534, the *New Living Translation* and likely many more translations either recognize only that Jesus was an offering for sin or give that rendering as an alternate. The Jewish sin offering was called simply "sin." It is a horrible error to think otherwise because you would miss that Jesus is an offering from God to come live in us and cleanse us from sin (I Jn. 1:7, I Jn. 1:9) and change us into his likeness (II Cor. 3:18).

As a offering for sin, Jesus gave himself, his life or soul (biblical "blood"), to come and live in men through the Spirit and bring them up into his likeness (II Cor. 3:18, I Cor. 15:49, Rom. 8:29) as mature sons of God. **He is doing that work now.**

"Christ also suffered for us leaving us an EXAMPLE for" us **to follow his steps [do what he did]**" (I Pet. 2:21). Immediately before his sweating blood in Gethsemane and then his rejection and crucifixion, Jesus said that James and John would drink of the same cup of rejection and crucifixion that he was about to endure (Mt. 20:23): they would do the same thing he was about to do. Paul, as we have noted, wrote that we are to have the same mind as Christ to be "obedient unto death, even the death of the cross" (Phil. 2:8); and Peter tells us to "arm" ourselves "with the same mind" as Christ who suffered for us in the flesh (I Pet. 4:1). Christ was our **example, not a substitutive** victim. He is the pioneer (K.J.V. "captain") of our salvation (Heb. 2:10). We all are to do what he did. That is what salvation is about. We either do it or we live in a delusion and miss what Jesus really did and is doing.

We could not follow Jesus to do an expiatory "work on the cross;" and Jesus did not do one either. What he did on the cross was to (1) bear the sin of our blameworthy hatred for him and for God and show it to us and to the world (Jn. 15:24), (2) get crucified and resurrect in the eyes of the whole world and return in Spirit baptism in many, (3) suffer for us leaving us an "EXAMPLE" that we "should follow his steps" as thousands have (I Pet. 2:21), and (4) be "declared to be the Son of God with power...by the resurrection from the dead" (Rom. 1:4) after men killed him and God raised him. (5) "God commends his love toward us in that while we were yet sinners Christ died for us" (Rom. 5:8) (to be an example to us and to come live **IN us**). He was not just talk: he did what he preached and what is necessary for us, which may be being "faithful unto death" (Rev. 2:10, 6:9, 12:11, I Jn. 3:16).

If we avoid and circumvent reality, we can have a delusional confidence in Jesus as being a substitute by his doing every hard thing for us: and we will miss the kingdom of God and take the path to destruction. Many love scripture translations and preachers who tell them that God wants them to have natural comfort and pleasures and that only Jesus had to be made "perfect through sufferings" (Heb. 2:10). They thank God for what Jesus did not do. Those likely will have a rude awakening.

However, if we do not reject Jesus as our "example" (I Pet. 2:21) to be followed and as our leader (K.J.V. "captain" Heb. 2:10) who was the first to do what his followers must do so they can be like him and receive the place in God and the rewards God has designed for them, we must be pressing into the kingdom of God (Lk. 16:16) and finding and taking the pressed-in gate and narrow way that leads to life (Mt. 7:14) and overcome (Rev. 3:21). We need to avoid and hate the wide gate and broad way leading to destruction that "many" take (Mt. 7:13). We choose.

Jesus was a "show-and-tell" of God (Emmanuel or "God with us," Mt. 1:23, Isa. 7:14) and of a son of God, a maturing or mature child of God. He was made "in all things" "like unto his brethren" (Heb. 2:17) and was made "perfect through sufferings" (Heb. 2:10) and "learned" "obedience by the things which he suffered" (Heb. 5:8). Jesus "was in all points tempted like as we are" (Heb. 4:15). If he had been made differently from us or had advantages that are not offered to us or was tempted differently than we are tempted, we could not expect to be made like him; but we are to be like Jesus (Rom. 8:29, I Cor. 15:47-49, II Cor. 3:18). "He that says he abides in him ought himself" to walk "even as he walked" (I Jn. 2:6).

Jesus has overcome and come back to live in us and coach us as we overcome and "work out" our "salvation with fear and trembling" (Phil. 2:12). "And being made perfect [or "perfectly qualified"], he became the author of eternal salvation unto all them that <u>obey</u> him [not to all them who intellectually believe in him or preach him or rejoice]" (Heb. 5:9). He is our "<u>forerunner</u>" who has gone into what is called the "Holy of Holies" (Heb. 6:19,20).

Note that it is Jesus' soul or life that saves us. It is doing that <u>now</u>; and **we are being created in the image of God now** if we are participating with our Shepherd and Lord. His body or natural blood would have been a small sacrifice compared to his eternally giving himself to bring up the whole creation into the glorious liberty of the sons of God. Thousands have been crucified for their faithfulness to God: Jesus was their and our "example" and forerunner.

Jesus has God's love that caused him to fully give himself "for our sins [errors, failures and rebellions] THAT HE MIGHT DELIVER US FROM THIS PRESENT EVIL WORLD" with its darkened understandings (Gal. 1:4). He came to "bear witness unto the truth" (Jn. 18:37) and thereby "destroy the works of the devil" (I Jn. 3:8) and "deliver them" who feared death (Heb. 2:15). Our salvation is that we escape the "corruption that is in the world through lust [our lusts]" (II Pet. 1:4). We need to be saved <u>from ourselves</u>, from "fulfilling the desires of the flesh and of the mind" (Eph. 2:3) "according to the course of this world, according to the prince of the power of the air, the spirit that now works in the children of disobedience" (Eph. 2:2). "For Christ also has once suffered for sins, the just for the unjust, **that he might bring us to**

God" (I Pet. 3:18). Jesus "came" "to call" "sinners" to repentance (Mk. 2:17).

"His own self bare our sins in his own body on the tree" (I Pet. 2:24): our crucifying him is "our sins." Now men are condemned in their own eyes for having the nature to have "both seen and hated both" Jesus and his "Father" (Jn. 15:24) and then crucified Jesus. He revealed to us that we hated God while we were self-deceived that we were good people and were friendly toward God. We can still praise God and yet be disobedient and ungodly people. We can have peace and joy but not righteousness; and we will be one item short of the kingdom of God (Rom. 14:17). Jesus bore our hatred on the cross, but did not bear our other sins. Men now are still hating God by hating Christians in whom He lives and His Word, His ruling men, and righteousness.

I Pet. 2:24 says: "By whose stripes ye were healed." How? The next verse (verses were made in A.D. 1551) says: you "are now returned unto the Shepherd and Bishop or your souls" (I Pet. 2:25). It is spiritual healing. Repentance is spiritual healing. Jesus said: "They that are whole have no need of the physician, but they that are sick. I came not to call the righteous, but sinners to **repentance**" (Mk. 2:17).

The whole antichrist nonsense about Jesus' death and natural blood being the agents that propitiated God when He was supposedly offended with men has confused and misdirected multitudes. If God needed to be propitiated, then Jesus was lying when he said that to be like God we needed to love our enemies. God loves His enemies (Mt. 5:43-48) and does not change (Mal. 3:6). He has no hatred in Him because He is light (I Jn. 1:5) and hatred is darkness (I Jn. 2:11). If God needed to be propitiated, then He would not be God. The thoughts that God could or needed to be propitiated or liked blood are thoroughly pagan and foreign to Old and New Testament thought and writings. A God who already loves you cannot be propitiated: He is already fully propitious toward you and always has been. Someone would be in delusion and insensitivity to what is illogical if he wanted God who is love and actively loves even His enemies to be propitiated.

There are those that believe the substitution gospel heresy is supported by the Old Testament sacrificial system. Many believe that the O.T. sacrifices that "made" "remembrance" "of sins" (Heb.

10:3) brought about the forgiveness of sins. Any biblical scholar will tell you that that is not so. The O.T. sacrifices "covered" sins but did not remove them. The O.T. system was substitutive because God did not want men to die physically for the things to which the sacrifices called attention. Heb. 10:4 and 10:11 tell us that "it is not possible that the blood of bulls and goats should take away sins." The sacrifices were "the ministration of death" and "the ministration of condemnation" (II Cor. 3:7,9). They did not justify anyone: "by the deeds of the law there shall no flesh be justified in His [God's] sight" (Rom. 3:20). The New Covenant, a "ministration of righteousness" ministered by the Spirit (II Cor. 3:9,8), has nothing like the O.T. legal sacrifices. The sacrifices do not now take place in a substitute. Sacrifices do take place in the hearts of the individuals who die to themselves and live spiritually by the life of Jesus who lives by God (Jn. 6:57). "The sacrifices of God are a broken spirit, a broken and a contrite heart" (Ps. 51:17).

False teaching and bad translations have blindfolded and misdirected multitudes. It all takes place in bad "churches" that are unlike the real church. They misdirect and deceive their people and insist on unity in their heresies. They know nothing of abiding in the living Lord and Shepherd and being the kingdom of God and individually hearing Jesus' voice and having the anointing that teaches us all things. They know nothing about not following a stranger (Jn. 10:5): they follow anyone who has his collar on backwards or attracts crowds. Some are fraternities bonded together by supporting their agreed upon delusions that keep them from having to each responsibly live to and obey God.

"Churches" are the major enemies and competitors to the kingdom of God that Jesus and his apostles and teachers preached and taught. There are false teachers, false apostles, false brethren, false Christs, false prophets, and false churches. We need to "try the spirits whether they are of God, because MANY false prophets [people who claim to speak for God] are gone out into the world" (I Jn. 4:1). "Wherefore by their fruits [what they do] you shall know them" (Mt. 7:20). "Prove all things" (I Thes. 5:21).

It was never God who had to be changed. It was man; and many a man has welcomed the antichrist delusion that he does not need to be radically changed and that Jesus did what was necessary, that God is not going to change each man into the image

49

of God. Many refuse to die to their old selves and yet sit in church meetings pretending to be like those beside them that are denying themselves and living to Jesus (II Cor. 5:15). If you take Jesus as your Lord, all that you have and all you are, are at his disposal. Your home is God and you come to know the truth that He owns you (Ez. 18:4). Your real identity is with God, not with men.

Jesus "gave himself [and is giving himself now]," not gave just his mortal body or natural blood, to "deliver us from this present evil world" (Gal. 1:4). We were not **bought with a price**" (I Cor. 6:20, I Cor. 7:23). Who were we "bought" from? God already owned "all souls" (Ez. 18:4). We are not Jesus' until WE are choosing continually to live to him. Rightly translated, we are **paid for,** but **not bought,** by his sacrifices to show us God and come live in us and save us.

Likewise, Jesus was **not a ransom** in the way most people think. He was a ransom in the sense that you might ransom an automobile from a car lot by giving money for it. Jesus was and is a price or ransom (Greek *lutron* and *antilutron* for "looser") that Jesus and God are paying to bring men up to be sons of God as God planned to do from the first of the creation (Mt. 20:28, Mk. 10:45, I Tim. 2:6). Jesus gave and gives his life not to be an ordinary ransom for many, but to be a looser, a savior from sin (error, failure, or rebellion).

We must have "escaped the corruption that is in the world through lust [<u>our</u> over-desire]" (II Pet. 1:4). It is we that were living "in the vanity of" our minds with our "understanding darkened," "alienated from the LIFE of God through ignorance," with "blindness" of "heart" (Eph. 4:17.18). We must be regenerated from <u>our</u> degenerate minds and desires that separate us from God and His righteousness. Jesus suffered to bring us to God (I Pet. 3:18). That comes as we are "not conformed to this world" but we are being "transformed by the renewing of" our "mind" (minds) and are in union with Christ who is living in us and we are being healed spiritually because we have returned to the "Shepherd and Bishop of" our "souls" (I Pet. 2:25). We have the problems for which we ourselves must find the real solution, the narrow way that leads to life that "few there be that find it" (Mt. 7:14), the path directed by Christ. We find when we are seeking and obeying God.

We have emotional injuries that need healing. We need to forgive all people so that we can be forgiven. We can be freed from guilt for our mistakes and misdeeds when we believe that God's offer and desire, which is for Him to "forgive" people or get rid of their sins and sin nature, is for all people for here and now and in the "hereafter." We may need little or much healing. Jesus will do it all if we listen to him, wait and follow him. God will give wisdom to any man who keeps asking Him (Ja. 1:5-8). Jesus rescues people from deep wounds that warp their abilities to (1) understand their needs and to (2) want to be liberated.

We need to live with a "good conscience" toward God (Heb. 10:2, I Tim. 1:5,19, Heb. 13:18, I Pet. 3:16,21) and not a conscience that fails and needs "altar calls" or a conscience that agrees with Satan, "the accuser of our brethren," who accuses us "before our God day and night" as we come before God in prayer and love (Rev. 12:10).

Do you experience rejection when you go to God in prayer? Do you suppose discouragement is coming from Satan and not from God who wants you to overcome Satan with the word of God that says: (1) "Let us come boldly to the throne of grace, that we may obtain mercy, and find grace to help in time of need" (Heb. 4:16) and says (2) "ask [or "be asking"] and it shall be given you, seek and you shall find, knock and it shall be opened unto you" (Mt. 7:7) and says (3) "God is love"? Faith is having confidence in God's promises, "great and precious promises, that by these you might be partakers of the divine nature having escaped the corruption that in the world through lust" (II Pet. 1:4).

A sexual desire coming into our mind when we see a physically attractive person should not be allowed to nest; however, it should not be thought to be sinful. Jesus was "in all points tempted like as we are" (Heb. 4:15). He had sexually lustful thoughts, but was "without sin" (Heb. 4:15). Men and women have "lusts" that they can allow to conceive and produce sin which produces spiritual death, separation from God (Ja. 1:14,15, Isa. 59:2). When a person in his or her heart is willing to commit sexual sin, sin has conceived: he or she has been looking on a woman or man for the purpose of wanting to commit sexual sin and will do so if he or she has the opportunity (see Mt. 5:28). But Satan lies to you that a lust, a desire, is a sin in itself even if you

51

are resisting it. Well, Satan is a liar and "the accuser of our brethren" (Rev. 12:10) and will have a party in condemning you if you let him. Satan tempted Jesus with all kinds of sin in the wilderness (Lk. 4:1,2), during the 3 years of his ministry dealing with church authorities and his apostles (Mt. 16:23, Jn. 8:44), and during the years before his recorded ministry. Satan got all kinds of things into Jesus' mind, and Jesus rejected them. Jesus said Satan "hath nothing in me" (Jn. 14:30). Jesus was "without sin" (Heb. 4:15), he did not submit to temptations.

The phony gospel tells you that you can have forgiveness for sins and go to "heaven" if you believe Jesus was a sacrifice as a substitute for your being punished forever. However, God and scriptures tell you that you will have taken care of your sins when you repent with your whole being so that you are a changed new person doing and trying to do what is right. Scriptures say God was forgiving sins before and during Jesus' earthly ministry so that Jesus' death and shed blood were and are not at all needed for forgiveness of sins. Jesus said God had no pleasure in sin sacrifices patterned after those done under the law; and that he came instead to do God's will, which replaced dealing with sin by acknowledging sins by killing a victim. God says He is the savior of all men and will some day be all in all, everything in everything. God forbade substitutive death for another's sins and said additionally that each man should die for his own sin; and that death to our "old man" and water baptism burial of the "old man" saves us from ourselves (I Pet. 3:21). Anselm in A.D. 1098 invented the utterly stupid and unscriptural substitution teaching that has destroyed much or most authentic Christianity.

It is not about God being offended by your having sinned. God expects all men will sin: and our job, as was Jesus' (Isa. 7:15, Heb. 1:9), is to learn to live intelligently to hate sin and love good and overcome sin. It is not a done deal for each of us: we must each learn to love good and hate evil. The scriptures say that sinning destroys you and is stupidity when it is volitional rather than ignorance. Being born again so you are doing God's will, are led by the Spirit, are following the man Jesus who is our Shepherd, and are in God's kingdom or control is the only way you will experience heaven and God's life, be "saved" (Heb. 5:9) and be righteous and not be continuing in sin.

God forbids that a substitute die for another's sin in Deut. 24:16 and Jer. 31:30. And in those two verses He also says that "every man shall be put to death for his own sin" and "every one shall die for his own iniquity" (and this happens when a person becomes "dead" as in Rom. 6:7 and is born again and made a "new creature" and buries his "old man" in water baptism). He said: "For I desire mercy and NOT SACRIFICE: and the knowledge of God [Jn. 17:3] more than burnt offerings" (Hos. 6:6, Mt. 9:23, 12:7). God wanted and wants us to accept "the knowledge of God," His being "merciful to" our "unrighteousness" (Heb. 8:12, Ex. 34:6,7) without any sacrifices of animals or a man being involved. The first thing God describes Himself to Moses as being His nature, is "merciful" (Ex. 34:6). The acceptance of God's being merciful is a **vital** part of our having "the knowledge of God" (Hos. 6:6, Jn. 17:3) which God desires and which is the "life eternal" Jesus expressed in Jn. 17:3. Mic. 6:6-8 speaks similarly. Receiving God's mercy destroys our arrogance, keeps us connected to God, and allows us to admit our errors and wrong and ask help from God to change our hearts and "cleanse" us from ALL sin and unrighteousness (I Jn. 1:7,9).

It allows God to treat us as dear children who are learning from Him, looking to Him, trusting in Him and knowing Him as He is as our dear Father (Gal. 4:5,6). We are not accepted by Him because of our righteousness but because He loves us. It is quite a different relationship from that of knowing God as being a tyrant giving laws and our being under schoolmasters (Gal. 3:24) and tutors (Gal. 4:2).

Heb. 10:5,6,8 and Ps. 51:16 tell us God had no pleasure in sacrifices and offerings "which are offered by the law" or in "sacrifice and offering and burnt offerings and offering for sin." Heb. 10:7 and 10:9 speak of Jesus saying that he replaces sacrifices and offerings by doing God's will: "he takes away the first [sacrifice and offering] that he may establish the second [doing the will of God]." Jesus is saying God did not desire and he did not come to be anything like a sacrifice that was offered under the law; but he came to give God obedience, which is better than just recognizing sin. We now are to live like Jesus lived (I Jn. 2:6).

The ideas that God is angry in more than an anthropomorphic sense, are misdirecting the thinking of

53

multitudes. God does not actually forgive sins (p. 35). He sends them away and looses men from them when they repent, and only when they repent or are changed. Childish imaginative explanations about how God feels about men are stupid and blasphemous. God never hated anyone except in an anthropomorphic sense. He loves His enemies and He is love and will eventually save everyone and be "all in all." He has good plans for each of His "offspring."

The phony gospel is from Satan who "deceives the whole world" (Rev. 12:9, Isa. 14:13-17). It is blasphemy. Its aim is to derail a man from knowing God and to make him a sin-enslaved servant to his "old man," his natural carnal self, and make him a stranger to the kingdom of God. It produces thankfulness for a delusional salvation and keeps men from the strait gate and narrow path of obedience to and participation in Christ. It puts men on the wide path that leads to destruction because it does not require the things Jesus taught. It is a substitute for real Christianity, a cheap imitation. It is revolting to many who seek God.

Those who have been deceived to trust it need to see the heresy for what it is and see that they are destroying their souls by embracing a false gospel and that their example is misleading others. They need to fear it and leave false churches and discontinue fellowshipping with those who insist on embracing it after they have been shown the truth of the kingdom of God.

Men are held captive to the phony gospels by fear, (1) fear of the unknown and (2) the fear that clergy might be right in saying that if we do not believe and act on what they say, we will end up in unthinkable and never ending torture in hell. That kind of intimidation has been used by the Roman Catholic Church to tremendously enrich itself by fleecing their sheep for the claimed purpose of praying members' relatives out of suffering in the imaginary purgatory.

Now before leaving talking about the false, polluted, diseased gospel that has caused an epidemic, it is needed that we consider the wrong meaning of the "forever and ever" and also the false ideas about "hell," both of which fuel the phony gospel or gospels.

4

For Ever and Ever

Why would anyone say "for ever and ever"? Is it stronger language to say "for ever and ever" than to say "for ever"?

No. It is nonsensical! It is like: "for good and for good."

But then look at Dan. 7:18: "But the saints of the Most High shall take the kingdom, and possess the kingdom for ever, even for ever and ever." Again, the translation makes no sense. It has 3 *evers* repeating themselves. We may justify it by saying it is a tradition to accept it and that we are guessing it is showing emphasis; but, we will pay a heavy price for our regarding God's word to us with such lightness and irresponsibility.

A translation or Bible version is men's ideas of God's word; and translators, who may be fine scholars and experts in languages, may make their translations say anything but what God would have us know. If you accept any phrase of translation as being the correct one without your being shown by God that it is so, it is much like making yourself an idol. Being a Greek scholar is not being a spiritually enlightened translator. Some K.J.V. translators helped burn two men at the stake and disfigure and nearly kill a Baptist minister. Translators often unintentionally or as propaganda "pull the wool" over the eyes of the reader and block his sight by not giving alternate meanings to those that they choose. It is like erecting false street signs that misdirect.

Interpretation, not translation, is most of their work; and some translators are most unqualified to interpret. They may cover up the true meanings completely. Many are steeped in traditions that no one has questioned and changed for many hundreds of years.

We should be outraged with a holy outrage that translators are more interested in their own opinions and accepted traditions than with faithfully transmitting the whole truth and nothing but the truth so that we, not them, can make decisions about what is right. The "anointing" "teaches" US "of all things" (I Jn. 2:27). We should "prove all things" and "hold fast that which is good" (I

Thes. 5:21). This is especially true in regard to translations or Bible versions because your light is darkness when you believe a mistranslation is the word of God when it is the opposite of truth. Translation is nothing like a precise science.

Robert Young of *Young's Concordance* and *Young's Literal Translation of the Bible* cautions that we need to know the languages in which the scriptures were written down. Most cannot: many will not even deny themselves and spend hours seeking true meanings of scriptures.

We need translations, not opinions that masquerade as translations or translations of thought, as many pretend to give us. Translators handle or mishandle God's word. Recognizing this, the 1901 A.S.V. was called the "Rock of Bible Honesty."

Dan. 7:18 in the Rotherham's *Emphasized Bible* says: "shall receive the kingdom and shall possess the kingdom for the age, yea, for the age of ages." Now that does not sound as pretty as the K.J.V. "for ever, even for ever and ever;" however, people who know what is at stake and what the language literally says do not agree that the K.J.V.'s pretty translations are necessarily anything but falsehoods in their treatments of *eternal, everlasting, for ever, and for ever and ever.* Vincent's *Word Studies in the New Testament, Cruden's Concordance, Vines Expository Dictionary of Old and New Testament Words, Young's Concise Critical Bible Commentary,* the *Concordant Literal New Testament,* Rotherham's *Emphasized Bible,* and many other sources indicate the fallacy in believing that translations as *eternal, everlasting, for ever,* and *for ever and ever* are necessarily correct translations. There may not be any "for ever" or "for ever and ever" or "everlasting" in the original writings: and what a great difference that can make to our understandings of scripture.

Literal translations of what are usually translated *eternal* or *everlasting,* are *age-during* or *age-abiding.* They may, though, be references to God as the Eternal One or Everlasting One.

An age is a time in which something gets done. Aristotle used it of a man's lifespan. What it means in scriptural use is vitally important, not clear, and likely different in different situations or for different people.

Since we know that God "is the savior of all men," Jesus is the mercy seat or propitiatory for the sins of the whole world, all

56

men will be made alive in Christ as all died in Adam, all are alive to God now and Jesus preached to those who died in or before the flood, Sodom will be restored, every knee shall bow, God will be all in all, and all Israel will be saved since it was God Himself who concluded them in unbelief so that He could have mercy on them (Rom. 11:32), we know that *eternal, everlasting, for ever* and *for ever and ever* are often dangerous, misleading, false translations that contradict many scriptures whose translations are not in question.

Suppose that you read and believe that "the devil that deceived them was cast into the lake of fire and brimstone where the beast and the false prophet are, and shall be tormented day and night for ever and ever" (K.J.V. Rev. 20:10). You would miss the literal translation you would find in an interlinear Greek-English New Testament or literal translations such as those by Young or Rotherham which all say "to" or "unto" "the ages of ages." And suppose it is just saying "into times of times." We still do not know what is being said. It might be that "times of times" refers to periods of correction as "seven times shall pass over you" in Daniel 4:25,32 applied to the times in which Nebudchadnezzar would undergo heart changes and learn that God is running things. "From glory to glory" (II Cor. 3:18) may be what is meant by "for ever and ever." Whatever it means, we have overwhelming and repeated scriptural testimony that God will eventually save all men and be "all in all" and have no fire in His basement.

5

Hell

There are people who are stunted spiritually because they have been harmed by others and have not forgiven them, have not given up judging them and wishing them ill treatment. They deal with their hurt and console themselves by assuring themselves that their persecutors will become victims and receive the pain they received or maybe much more and with no end ever. Some are unable to do anything about bitterness that has sprouted up in them. It can be very hard and take years to overcome betrayal or infidelity that has destroyed or radically changed much of your life. Victims may have perceived needs to believe in retribution by God and that they will never meet their abusers again.

There are others who think they are doing God a favor by intimidating men to believe their propaganda about God's having an evil side of Himself that will torture people forever if they do not do what they claim God says. There are those that think that the fear of an unending torture is the only thing that brings a man to God. There are others that see that this opinion is keeping men from knowing Jesus and God and is opposing God's purpose "in Christ" to be "reconciling the world unto Himself" (II Cor. 5:19). It is hard to be reconciled to a capricious god who might torture you for millions and millions of years because you made a wrong decision. What would you think of an earthly father who beat his child unmercifully every day year after year without any intention of ever doing any good to him or allowing his victim to escape?

Hell is a complicated subject because men have made it that way with their imaginations. It has been a great tool to enslave men to church leaders who are trusted to know the scriptures and to be God's special priests worthy of trust.

We have twice quoted a number of scriptures that say God will deal with people to save them after they leave their earthly bodies. No scripture rightly translated says that people cannot or will not be saved after they depart.

Many men make money and get honor and power by telling others they will go to hell if they do not have a salvation experience before they die; and many victims consequently have an isolated experience that is not much salvation and is a lot of misdirection.

Religious people often get misguided when they are intimidated with something that is wrong but seems to fulfill their wildest fears. Imaginations about hell and purgatory are great intimidators. We need to leave the door open for Jesus to modify our understandings because "if any man thinks that he knows any thing, he still knows nothing yet as he ought to know" (I Cor. 8:2), he has a lot to learn. We now "know in part" (I Cor. 13:12).

We have shown scriptures that say God will save all men and be "all in all." We have talked about *hell* in the *King James Version* Old Testament being the mistranslated *Sheol* and often in the K.J.V. New Testament a mistranslation of *Hades*. We have explained the wrong translations of *for ever, for ever and ever, eternal and everlasting*. We note here that there is a New Testament Greek manuscript word *aidios* that actually means "without end" that appears twice (Rom. 1:20; Jude 6) but not in conjunction with *hell*.

Rightly translated, *hell* is only in the New Testament. It is *gehenna* named for a valley and trash dump outside of Jerusalem where some think there were continual fires; and *gehenna* is the "lake of fire," "fire," and "furnace of fire." The lake of fire is located "in the presence of the holy angels" and "the Lamb [Jesus]" (Rev. 14:10, 20:10). God may be the fire that the ungodly feel. It may be the same as separation from intimacy with God or "outer darkness" where there is also "weeping and gnashing of teeth" (remorse) where go (1) some former "children of the kingdom" and (2) the wedding guest who had no wedding garment and (3) Jesus' wicked and slothful "Christian" servants (Mt. 8:12, 22:13, and 25:30). There is a place where there is weeping and gnashing of teeth that is not identified as outer darkness or fire but is a destination of (4) the "Christian" hypocrites and servants of Jesus who were to take care of his people but did the opposite (5) and many "Christians" who do not "enter in at the strait [narrow] gate" (Mt. 24:51, Lk. 13:24-28). "Wailing [same Greek word as for *weeping* above] and gnashing of teeth" is for (6) the "children of the wicked one" in Jesus' kingdom (church) that will go into the "furnace of fire" and for (7) "the wicked" that will be separated from the just and put into the "furnace of fire" at the end of the age (K.J.V. "world") (Mt. 13:38-42, 47-50). Age-during fire "prepared for the devil and his angels [*angels* means *messengers*, human messengers or spirit messengers or both]" is a place where (8) Christians and others will go if they have neglected to feed the hungry, clothe the naked, take care of (K.J.V. "visit") the sick and imprisoned, give shelter to strangers and give drink to the thirsty (Mt. 25:41-46).

(9) Christians and others who have bad habits, an eye or foot or hand (how they judge or lust, how they "walk" or behave, actions they take) that cause them to sin and which they allow, will go into hell (*gehenna*) (Mt. 5:29,30, Mt. 18:9). Many U.S. "Christians" may go to hell due to voluntary addiction to internet sex. In Mt. 10:28, Jesus tells us to not fear those who can kill the body but not the soul; but to fear Him that can "destroy both soul and body in hell." Literally, he said: "take away well being" in hell.

Hell is real. It may be that an abuser of children will spend a lot of "ages" or "times" in the embarrassing presence "of the Holy angels and of the Lamb" (Rev. 14:10) without any ability to change his situation or control anything. He may go through agony and remorse and weep and gnash his teeth as his life is an open book and he and others are made aware of the harm he has done and how despicable he is. He may experience "our God" who is "a consuming fire" and love (Heb. 12:29, Deut. 4:24). Love may be a very hot consuming fire to a person who hates and is totally selfish. To bring him to full repentance, the sufferer's sufferings may be more or less than the sufferings he has caused. He may be more or less responsible due to whether or not he were brought up like Saddam's 2 sons who were forced as young children to take guns and shoot caged men or he was a Christian who stubbornly made bad decisions. Jesus' servants (church people) who knew to do well and did not do well will be beaten a lot; those who were ignorant and did wrong will receive little correction (Lk. 12:47,48). Jesus does not say that any will get unceasing correction.

There are different kinds of fire. People with no human bodies could not be subject to natural fire and be weeping because of natural burning. Their selfishness and meanness could be consumed and corrected by the spiritual fire of God, God Himself.

Gideon's son Jotham prayed: "let fire come out from Abimelech and devour the men of Shechem and the house of Millo; and let fire come out from the men of Shechem and from the house of Millo and devour Abimelech" (Judges. 9:20). Abimelech then fought against the men of Shechem and killed them; and a lady in a tower in another city dropped part of a mill stone on Abimilech's head and killed him. Those were the "fires" that Jotham prayed for.

The fires of hell seem to be characterized by "outer darkness" and something that makes people have remorse and repentance and weep and gnash their teeth. Ordinary fire does not make you weep and gnash your teeth: it makes you scream with pain.

We do not need to engage in saying we know more than the little we do know about hell. It definitely is not a final destination, as God will later be all in all and everyone will be made alive in Christ Jesus etc. It is not hatred from God because we know God loves His enemies (Mt. 5:43-45). It has to be a remedy that changes those repenting folks who will be weeping and gnashing teeth in remorse. Punishment meted out in love is for correction and seems to be appropriate to the degree of knowledge and culpability the participant has (Lk. 12:47,48, I Pet. 1:17, Rev. 20:12,13). The people who undergo hell seem to be stubborn, irresponsible, disobedient and deliberately ungodly, as are many "Christians." It may well be that the average lukewarm churchgoer will need more correction in hell than Hitler. God will correct men according to His judgment.

We note that Rev. 20:11-15 tells of the great "white throne judgment" where men are judged out of the books (probably records in their minds-Rom. 2:15,16) and the book of life (possibly Jesus' mind for those who are in Jesus). This is not a final judgment, though many who do not love their enemies assume and rejoice in the belief that it is a final judgment. People are judged "according to their works" (Rev. 20:13, Rom. 2:6), not just tossed into fire with every bad person. There is no "one size fits all" in an imaginary unending punishment in fire. It appears that various works get appropriate treatment. God is love.

And Rev. 21:8 says: "But the fearful, and unbelieving, and the abominable, and murderers, and whoremongers, and sorcerers, and idolaters, and all liars, shall have their part in the lake which burns with fire and brimstone: which is the second death." It does not suggest the fire and brimstone will not do their work destroying carnality and then release corrected souls to enjoy the kingdom of God. As flesh burns in natural fire, carnality may burn in the lake of fire.

Some preachers ignorantly imagine how hot, painful and lasting the fire will be. They torment people with their imaginations. It certainly will be deadly serious to fall into God's hands. It also will be blessed. We do not know what God's fire will be like. We know it will cause remorse.

Fire is a purifier. God takes away what is wrong so that what is right can live. God weeds His garden. God does what is love, what is necessary. It is painful to a person to lose addictions and wrong thinking that he has depended upon. It is very painful to a person to have to leave a church out of which God is calling him so that he can find God and come into God's kingdom; and many refuse to obey God in this regard. It is painful to be weak and learn to trust in Jesus with your whole life. It is painful to begin living to God and not to the approval of men, or of your wife or family or even your own self (Lk. 14:26). "We must through much tribulation enter into the kingdom of God [through many hardships be entering into being controlled by God]" (Acts 14:22). Jesus speaks of our need to "count the cost" (Lk. 14:28) of our entering into participation in the kingdom voluntarily. The "lake of fire" may be what will convince the unwilling, irresponsible and stubborn to give up the darkness they are in and reach out and pay the price to come into the joy of the kingdom. "Christians" who are not finding and doing God's will should fear.

God will cause all His works, His creations and His destructions, to praise Him (Ps. 145:10). Those who understand what He has done and is doing, will praise Him. You must be "born again" to be seeing "the kingdom of God" (Jn. 3:3) and appreciate what God is doing. You must be "pure in heart [motive]" to be seeing God (Mt. 5:8). Suffering is involved for those He is bringing through metamorphosis "from glory to glory" (Acts 14:22, II Cor. 3:18, Ro. 12:2). God "will not suffer you [allow you] to be tempted above that you are able, but will with the temptation also make a way to escape [He is in control and may test you greatly but not more than you can bear and He has provided an exit strategy]" (I Cor. 10:13). And "the sufferings of this present time are not worthy to be compared with the glory that shall be revealed in us" (Rom. 8:18).

6

Churches

The biblical Greek word for church is *ecclesia*, a called out assembly. God does the calling and we do the assembling. Jesus said: "For where 2 or 3 are gathered together in my name, there am I in the midst of them" (Mt. 18:20). Wow!! Jesus tells us a place we should find him.

There is church, greatly anointed, excellent, desirable church that may not be appreciated for its value. There Christ is active just as you get a flame when you bring two glowing coals together. You need 2 or 3 participating in Jesus. 2 or 3 without Jesus' participating in the members is not church. We must highly reverence and heed Mt. 18:20.

Today, few people know what a church is, a called out people participating in Jesus. They usually think of a building with a pastor or other officer and do not know the church is the building in which God resides, and that that building is a divine construction of men who are all "lively stones" (I Pet. 2:5). When you are asked where your church is, you can tell people that they looking at your church, that your church goes home after a meeting, and Jesus is your church's headquarters. In calling their meeting houses churches, many "churches" profane the name church.

The way a church meeting should go is described by Paul in I Cor. 14:26-31. Paul writes: "How is it then brethren? When you come together, every one of you has a psalm [inspired song], has a doctrine [teaching], has a tongue [God-given anointed message in a strange language], has a revelation [from God and Jesus His Son], has an interpretation [of the anointed strange language]." He says that there should be only 2 or 3 giving a message in a strange language and none speaking so unless there is an interpreter (verses 27,28). Is that your church? Why not?

He says "let the prophets speak <u>two or three</u>, and let the other [others] judge" (I Cor. 14:29). The prophets are people speaking for God, delivering inspired preaching under a Holy

Ghost anointing from God. No one should be speaking anything that is not under the inspiration of God. I Pet. 4:11 says speakers are to "speak as the oracles [mouth pieces] of God." We should not accept any less. Preaching must be careful faithfulness to God. No preacher should receive any glory from men. It is vital that authentic preaching be and be recognized as coming from God. God should receive glory for His ministering through members.

There should never be just one person preaching. That is a destructive, traditional, widespread, intolerable, ungodly disorder from which we should run. And the other people are to evaluate what is being taught. And "If any thing be revealed to another that sits by [evaluating], let the first hold his peace" (I Cor. 14:30). If God reveals something to someone who is listening and evaluating, the one preaching, who should be expecting that it can and will happen, should stop and have the man or woman to whom God is showing something tell what God is showing. The listeners must be ready and willing to bring a revelation. It is the responsibility of each hearer to be listening and ready to give a revelation Jesus might want to be brought.

Anything else is setting Jesus "at naught" (Mk. 9:12, Lk. 23:11) and devaluing most sisters and brethren as not being Jesus' ministers. Do you accept leaders practicing arrogant violence to Jesus and his people, the church?

You should never allow a leader to disrespect you as your not being inhabited by Christ and being a God-ordained priest or priestess of God (I Pet. 2:5,9, Rev. 1:6, Rev. 5:10, Ex. 19:6). You should never think of yourself as being less important than some man-ordained priest or as being less important to God than any other Christian. You have one lord, Jesus Christ. Members are "all" "brethren" (Mt. 23:8), never a "congregation." God Himself has structured it that way.

It is idolatry to have any other master than Jesus (Mt. 23:10) or to regard any man as your teacher (Mt. 23:8) in the sense that you follow a man's teaching rather than that you be responsible and "prove all things: hold fast that which is good" (I Thes. 5:21) and "try the spirits whether they are of God" (I Jn. 4:1). **You** have the **responsibility** to think and be judging with the help of the Holy Spirit (I Cor. 2:15). God does not treat us as children as He allowed the Israelites who refused to have God speak with them (Ex. 20:19) and demanded they hear only Moses (Ex.20:19). **We are commanded to seek and find truth for ourselves (Mt. 7:7,8).** <u>We are responsible for what we believe.</u> **If we will not hear and be led by the Holy Spirit and Jesus (I Jn. 2:27, Jn. 16.13, Jn. 10:27,28), we are refusing Jesus, God and God's kingdom: we are choosing delusions.**

"You may all prophesy one by one, that all may learn and all may be comforted" (I Cor. 14:31). It is normal that all prophesy often in church meetings. Church meetings without prophecy by many or all members are like buildings without lights. Do your meetings have lights?

Note that everyone has an active vocal ministry in a meeting though all are not always used in every meeting. Note that one person preaching is an ungodly disorder that limits or excludes Jesus who gives the anointing to teach and should not be confined to only one mouthpiece of men who are to "speak as the oracles [mouthpieces] of God" (I Pet. 4:11). Note that someone preaching is to be interrupted by any person who receives a revelation while the one preaching is talking. That is Jesus interrupting and it is Jesus' choice. That is God's kingdom. Anything else is disorder and often a performance and entertainment in which we should not participate. We MUST allow Jesus to speak with us through any member. It that your church?

None of us have anything we did not receive or anything to "glory" about as if we did not receive it (I Cor. 4:7). If this writer or any preacher or priest of God has anything worth saying, it did not come from himself but from God; and his ability to say it is also from God. And no one is great because God uses him. He is privileged to be used.

A preacher is not ever to be exalted. The "man Christ Jesus" is exalted because he is the active intermediary or "mediator between God and men" (I Tim. 2:5) who is actively mediating God (Lk. 10:22) and the New Covenant now (Heb. 8:6, 9:15, 12:24). The Covenant is God writing God's laws in men's minds and hearts and God's being God to women and men and causing all His people to be knowing the Lord for themselves "from the least to the greatest" (Heb. 8:10,11, Jer. 31:33,34). "There" is no "salvation in any other" than Jesus (Acts 4:12). Jesus has overcome to sit down with God in His throne (Rev. 3:21) and administrate His kingdom. Jesus now has been "given" "all power" "in heaven and in earth" (Mt. 28:18). He is our Shepherd (I Pet. 2:25, Jn. 10:11) who will help us "work out" our "salvation with fear and trembling" (Phil. 2:12). "Christ IN you" is your "hope of glory" (Col. 1:27). He is our Lord unto whom "all things [all in us and in others that opposes God] shall be subdued" (I Cor. 15:28) so that the kingdom of God will "break in pieces and consume" all other "kingdoms" and "stand for ever" (Dan. 2:44). He must be reverenced. He is God's administrator. God is fully in him (Col. 1:19). We are to obey him (Acts 3:22,23).

Men have spiritual and natural gifts that they often do not realize to have come from God; and that ignorance is very dangerous and can cause their souls to fall into conceit and to depart from living to and depending on God. None are greater than another except in the degree they serve others (Mk. 10:43,44, Mt. 23:11, 20:26,27). Jesus said also that whoever practices and teaches God's commandments will be called great in the kingdom of heaven (Mt. 5:19).

Some are temporarily more mature in some areas of development than others; but all are just "brethren" (Mt. 23:8, Rom. 8:29) being changed "from glory to glory" by the Holy Spirit (II Cor. 3:18) who is receiving from Jesus and ministering to each of us (Jn. 16:14). Christ's ministering through men is fantastic; however, much of the most important ministry to the body of Christ is done in prayer closets in secret. We have no right to exalt one person over another (Ja. 2:2-4); however, some "Christians" wrongly want to be exalted while the others are rightly refusing to take any glory from men. God has "tempered the body" such that "there should be no schism [division, discord] in the body, but that the members should have the same care one for another" (I Cor. 12:24,25). Is that your church?

A person must be great to God and not to men: "whose praise is not of men but of God" (Rom. 2:29, Jn. 5:44).

Paul writes: "For who makes you to differ from another? And what have you that you did not receive? Now if you did receive it, why do you glory as if you had not received it?" (I Cor. 4:7). There are gifted people and people who are temporarily further in maturity and wisdom than others; but there are no great men. Some men fill obvious needs that make them seem important to men; and some fill more important needs but are not recognized. Abraham Lincoln's life was serially a disaster before he became president. If you serve God without wanting credit from people, you are great in God's eyes, great in the kingdom of God (Mt. 23:11, Mk. 10:43,44), as you are if you DO and teach the commandments (Mt. 5:19). If you want honor from men, you are not serving God and will be "abased" (Mt. 23:11).

Note that each member in a church meeting can bring a prophecy (I Cor. 14:31) which is usually a message of (1) "edification [building up people]," (2) "exhortation [encouragement]," or (3) "comfort [comforting and reassuring people]" (I Cor. 14:3). *Prophesy* does not mean to tell the future: it means to speak for God whether or not it has anything to do with future events; and it should be judged by each member ("Prove [be testing] all things; hold fast that which is good"-I Thes. 5:21). A man's old mind, his "old man" and bias, can get into his prophecy. Satan can influence a prophecy. Men should be very careful to prophesy only what God is giving them; but, hearers should each judge and take hold only of what they know is Jesus.

It is impossible to print a program showing who will minister or what the topic of a meeting will be or what hymns will be sung. God does not tell people exactly whom He will use or what He is going to do. He may do the opposite of what they think God is telling them beforehand. He may anoint a person who has waited on him before a meeting, and then not use his ministry in that meeting. If you have a printed program or a time to end a meeting, you can be absolutely sure that God is being ignored.

The nature of the meeting is that God uses any or all members to participate in bringing His message to the church. Anyone who allows the meeting to be otherwise is opposing Jesus whether ignorantly or willfully. No one dominates and hogs the anointing. Jesus gets his message delivered through different members he anoints and inspires; and he can correct or add to any ministry by speaking through another ministry. Men can be very confident that they are not speaking a message from God when they are speaking from themselves and not from the anointing. Jesus can correct wrong teaching through other ministries who are in the Spirit and who will often be impressed when something is not right.

Where people meet and have only one preacher, Jesus has little access to minister to his body, the church, and to keep wrong teachings and biases from leading the sheep astray. Members of the body become malnourished and crippled from not fulfilling their ministries. The church gets warped and spiritually dies. Anything that is not growing is dead.

God does not endorse men because they go to a seminary or are politically shrewd with influential men. Christ comes to a meeting to supply "the effectual working in the measure of EVERY part" (Eph. 4:15,16), not the effectual working of a preacher and choir. The goal of a meeting is to hear from God and not to elevate men because of gifts God operates in them or because they have learned to sound good, wise, loud, or authoritative. Paul said: "I have planted, Apollos watered; but God gave the increase. So then neither is he that plants anything, neither he that waters; but God that gives the increase" (I Cor. 3:6,7).

Central of the church's goals is to love, help and respect the weaker members. Arrogance in leaders opposes and destroys the body of Christ. Arrogance is poison. Where members do not love one another with God's love, there is no church. Each must humble themselves with all others (I Pet. 5:5, Eph. 5:21) AND BE TOTALLY HONEST.

Where people are not baptized in the Spirit and living to Christ, an authentic church meeting is not possible. Members MUST be baptized in the Holy Spirit, must be living to God, and must be continually in the state of being born again so they are like the wind or the Spirit [Greek *pneuma* means "wind" or "spirit"] (Jn. 3:7,8). Where members are not "led by the Spirit" (Rom. 8:14) and their hearing and living to God does not exist, church meetings are like people sitting in the dark and listening to propaganda that is partly right and partly wrong and is destructive because it is polluted. You should not accept traditional, orthodox church; it is quite dead and it keeps Jesus from nourishing his body and gives his body delusions and spiritual gangrene from not having his blood (life) run through them. Thy shalt not have "pew potatoes."

The organized orthodox churches and many others have usurped Jesus: they have wrongly and arrogantly claimed the credentials of God for their ministers and have taught their people to honor them and not to live individually and directly to Jesus and

God. Absalom did similarly to take David's kingdom (II Chr. 15:1-6). They exalt men whom they select; and they hire their preferences as leaders and boycott Jesus' selections. God alone tempers the real church together and has given "more abundant honor to that part which lacked [honor], that there should be no schism [division] in the body, but that the members should have the same care one for another" (I Cor. 12:24,25). In song and speech, many churches give lip service to God, but their "hearts are far from" God (Isa. 29:13, Mt. 15:7,8).

Millions of Spirit Baptized Christians do not avail themselves of the Holy Spirit. They attend dead churches that are not Christ centered and Spirit controlled. They pray for God to occasionally manifest in their meetings instead of their always participating in Jesus and God. They have "revivals" because they are dead and altar calls because they do not live crucified lives to God at His altar. And they keep God out of their meetings so that they can run them like businesses and not need to wait on, trust and obey God. People attend for political, sexual, social, child education, financial, self-enhancement and other purposes.

Everyone should be of one mind that each member is Jesus' sheep and lives to Jesus as his Lord and to God and not to any men or organization of men (I Tim. 2:5, Rom. 14:4,8-10, Rom. 2:29, Mt. 7:1, Jn. 5:44). Members do not have to be at the same maturity or have the same beliefs. **They do have to be recognizing and serving Jesus as their lord; and they do need to be baptized in the Holy Spirit and helping and not damaging one another.**

"In the fear of God," they are to be "submitting" themselves "one to another" (Eph. 5:21). They are to listen to each other and communicate humbly and reverently, but not obey each other. Jesus' "commandment" is that we "love one another" as he loved us (Jn. 13:34, 15:12). You deal with Jesus when you interact with any one of his people. "Inasmuch as you have done it unto one of the least of theses my brethren you have done it unto me [Jesus]" (Mt. 25:40). How you treat an unattractive Christian is how you are treating Jesus. Your helping or ignoring one will get you to heaven or hell (Mt. 25:34,41).

Both younger and older are to submit to each other (no arrogance) (I Pet. 5:5). All, as we said above, are to be "submitting" themselves "to one another in the fear of God" (Eph. 5:21). The church cannot operate as Jesus' body unless every one of them is honored as a mouthpiece, partner and member of Jesus and listens responsively to other members. In Jesus' body, all are "members one of another" (Rom. 12:5, Eph. 4:25). They have the same Lord and life in them and interact with each other in Christ.

There are the tares, children of the devil (Mt. 13:38,39). We need to be discerning (Mt. 7:20) and judging the spirits.

Jesus said that if one Christian sins against another, the offended is to go to the offender and tell him his fault in private. If the other does not listen to him and respond appropriately, he is to take 2 or 3 witnesses so that every word of what is at question can be established. If the offender will not hear then, the offended is to take the matter to the whole church. And if the offender will not listen to the whole church (not just to some leaders), he is to be regarded as an outsider (Mt. 18:15-17). If this is not done, the church will suffer badly. It will have divisions.

An accused person must be heard thoroughly before being judged. Those judging must be **responsible** and make diligent inquiries and judge righteous judgment. There must be 2 witnesses of every accusation (Jn. 7:51, Deut. 1:16,17, 16:19, 19:15,18, Mt. 18:16, I Tim. 5:19). A false accuser or a judge showing partiality (judging irresponsibly) must be dealt with (I Tim. 5:21, Deut. 1:17, Deut. 19:18,19).

Also, if someone begins to worship and remembers that another Christian is offended with him, he is told to go be reconciled to him before worshipping (Mt. 5:23,24).

The leader of the church is Jesus. That must be inviolate. Christians must be baptized in the Holy Ghost to receive Jesus "IN" them (Jn. 14:17) and must treat Jesus as their Lord by obeying his written commandments and continual leading. They must make sure that he is reverenced and that he alone is the one being followed in their church and lives. If Jesus is not perceived as being the director and power in a church, the church is way off course and should halt and seek him until he is leading. Jesus commands we all be seeking (Mt. 7:7).

The church is operated by Jesus through the Holy Ghost. The Holy Spirit does what Christ directs him to do. He hears Jesus and does what Jesus has him do (I Cor. 12:7-11, Jn. 16:13,14,

Jn.15:26, Jn. 14:26) and not what men deem reasonable only to their natural shortsighted minds. Much "church" is men doing their wills and not knowing God's.

As soon as Christians cease to love and lay down their lives for their brethren (I Jn. 3:16), cease to live as members of Jesus by the leading of the Holy Spirit (Rom. 8:14), cease to obey Jesus' voice (Ex. 19:5, Jer. 7:23, Rev. 3:20, Rom. 8:14) and leadings (Jn. 10:27,28), do not deny themselves (Mk. 8:34), and do not recognize themselves as Jesus' body and members of each other (Rom. 12:5) and priests (Rev. 1:6), Jesus' body ceases to be his body.

Jesus may be knocking at the church door and saying: "I stand at the door and knock. If any man hear my voice, and open the door, I will come in to him and will sup [have spiritual communion] with him and he with me" (Rev. 3:20). Real church is where the individual members each are hearing Jesus' voice, having spiritual communion with him, and **obeying him**. There is always delusion where people each are not hearing and obeying Jesus their Lord.

Elders and deacons in a church are not ordained. They absolutely must come from in the local church and not any outside source (Acts 14:23, Titus 1:5). Paul and Barnabas and Titus did not "ordain" elders: in proper translation, they pointed out or appointed elders from the members. Paul and Barnabas were apostles or messengers of God that the Holy Spirit chose and were not chosen by apostolic succession or any human authorities (Acts. 13:1-3). Jesus operates the living church through the Holy Spirit. Paul stated he did not have authority over a church he had founded and nourished through Jesus for 18 months: "Not for that we have dominion [are dictators or masters] over your faith, but are helpers of your joy: for by faith you stand" (II Cor. 1:24). Jesus, not elders or apostles, is a churches' master.

Some designated faithful men need to responsibly oversee and minister to needs of the church and of its other ministers (all members are ministers and priests of God and should help; and deacons are there especially to help the elders serve the church). Some experienced men who depend on Christ to lead them must "be able by sound doctrine [teaching] both to exhort and to convince [convict] the gainsayers [those speaking in opposition]"

(Titus 1:9). They must stop men who want the preeminence (III Jn. 9), those bringing misleading teaching (I Tim.1:20, II Tim. 2:17, II Pet. 2:1-3, Gal. 1:7) and those who draw away followings after themselves (Acts 20:29,30). Paul told Timothy to publicly rebuke an elder who sinned, and not to neglect to do so (I Tim. 5:20,21).

The churches were given elders (older or experienced men- Acts 14:23; Acts 15:4,22,23; Acts 20:17,28, Ti. 1:5) or bishops (watchers, overseers-Phil. 1:1, Ti. 1:7) to serve the local churches. Elders and bishops are titles for the same ministries (Acts 20:17 and 28; Titus 1:5 and 1:7) but emphasize different aspects of pastoral qualification. They have to work together and be led by Christ since there are always a number of them in each assembly (Titus 1:5, Acts 14:23, Acts 20:17,28, Phil. 1:1). **No men in the New Testament are called pastors** although Eph. 4:11 literally translated says some men are given "as pastors," which refers to the pastoral role of elders (I Pet. 5:1-4, I Tim. 3:5).

Having only one elder or bishop (**or a "pastor"**) is a monumental disorder. Having a dominant elder would be the same as having only one elder except that the church would likely not know that there was a dominant elder and would be defrauded to believe that the other elders were authentic and not just deacons being called elders. Where elders are hypocrites, the church has a destroying virus.

There must be 2 or more elders in a church, as the scriptures indicate (Acts. 14:23, Phil. 1:1; Acts 15:4, Acts 20:17); and as we have insisted, the elders are pointed out in the local church and are not imported. They are not hirelings who would desert the flock if danger came; and they likely would not be paid unless their work prevented them from doing their regular jobs by which they were supporting their families. They cannot be fired and do not need to concern themselves with that. They could be removed because of sin. Paul was self-supporting (I Cor. 9:18, II Cor. 12:13) and said the fathers should care for the children and not vice versa (II Cor. 12:14).

Elders' jobs are for life (Rom. 11:29) and likely unpaid. They are not to do their elder's work for money (I Pet. 5:2). They are not to allow the church to be a "den of thieves" (Lk. 19:46) as greedy men and many orthodox leaders would have it to be. An elder (or bishop), **like every other member of the assembly**, has a full-time ministry as a member of Jesus' body. He likely supports himself and his family the same way other members of the church support their families. He is not over anybody though the K.J.V. translators distorted their translation to say that there were men over other men in the church. Acts 20:28 is a flagrant mistranslation in the K.J.V. and in some translations that copy the K.J.V.

An elder is to feed God's church and know and care for the members (I Pet. 5:1-4, I Tim. 3:5). But the members are to do the same. And an elder is to lead by being an example and not as a lord or boss over God's heritage (I Pet. 5:2,3). He is not to destroy the church by limiting Christ's working through other members. Such destroying is very common with men who become puffed up with self-importance and depose the Holy Spirit and monopolize or dominate ministering in meetings. Some think too much of themselves for them to believe that anyone could begin to rise up to follow their "examples" (I Pet. 5:3). Some arrogantly feel they are a head higher than others.

Jesus forbids any Christian should rule over others. Jesus said "the kings of the Gentiles exercise lordship over them; and they that exercise authority over them are called benefactors. But you shall not be so" (Lk. 22:25,26).

There is perhaps no more diabolic sin than that a person or group should believe that he or they have authority over other Christians or that he or they let others believe God has given them such authority.

The people and groups that participate in claiming authority over brethren are taking God's place and are erecting a temple veil by teaching others to deal with them in place of living directly to God. It is men spiritually kidnapping God's children from God. And it is widespread. It is as lethal to God's kingdom as a "worm" is to a computer. It is men refusing to allow Jesus to lead his people and to have his people obey his voice.

Taking a human leader or denomination or group as your authority is rejecting God the same as the Israelites demanded that Moses speak to them and that God not speak to them each directly (Ex. 20:19) and demanded a king and rejected God that He "should not reign over them" (I Sam. 8:7, 10:19). It is wholesale

75

destruction to the kingdom of God, the priesthood of all believers (I Pet. 2:5,9, Rev. 1:6, 5:10, Ex. 19:6), younger and older submitting to each other (I Pet: 5:5), members of Christ's body being "members one of another" (Eph. 4:25, Rom. 12:5), and men honoring that "God has tempered the body together having given more abundant honor to that part which lacked that there should be no schism [division] in the body but that the members should have the same care one for another" (I Cor. 12:24,25). God forbids men to temper His Son's body. Having both a priestly class and a lay class of Christians is an abomination and destruction of the kingdom of God.

This ugly evil of people approving of Christians ruling each other is supported by the K.J.V.'s wrong translations and those many translations that copied the K.J.V. It is how worldly governments and businesses are run. The K.J.V. translation was politically motivated to support the "divine right of kings" doctrine and to counter the *Geneva Bible.*

Translators who were or are not baptized with the baptism in the Holy Spirit and taught by the Holy Spirit would be unable to see how the church could operate with Jesus ruling it through the Holy Spirit and without a hierarchy of men directing and ruling it. Most people still cannot see that. Usually, the most greedy and politically savvy people rise to the top of a hierarchy. Hierarchies nourish heresies and **collusion among leaders** and ignore Jesus. They nourish ungodliness in leaders who begin to wrongly think themselves to be great as well as unaccountable to God or men. Silly men tell leaders they are great; and deceived leaders believe them and become abusive and arrogant and lose their place as Jesus' sheep and servants.

Leaders in denominations that have Spirit baptized members are sometimes greatly concerned about not violating criminal and civil law but not at all concerned about obeying Jesus' commands or loving or being just with their "brethren." They do not believe members are to have equal honor. We have seen some top "church" officers exposed in ungodly pursuits in recent months. A reputable recent pole found that many church leaders are addicted to internet sex, not to serving others and God.

The K.J.V. translates Heb. 13:17 to say: "Obey them that have the rule over you..." The "them that have the rule over you" is a mistranslation pure and simple. It should be "them that lead you," as many other versions and the Greek manuscript have it. And the "obey" is a mistranslation of a verb that means to "persuade" that is in the passive voice. *Vine's Expository Dictionary of Old and New Testament Words* says that matter is not about authority but is about a person being persuaded. It is not a matter of obeying fictitious "rulers." Peterson's *The Message* New Testament tells us to be responsibly listening to leaders rather than "obey" "rulers." *Young's Concise Critical Bible Commentary* has "have confidence in those leading you, and yield somewhat." Rotherham's *Emphasized Bible* says to be yielding to those guiding you. The *Concordant Literal New Testament* says men are to be persuaded by leaders. Leaders will give an account for their leading, not for the ways the sheep choose. People who take men as their rulers may be guilty of voluntary idolatry. **It is impossible to obey men and God and thus "serve 2 masters"** (Mt. 6:24, I Tim. 2:5) regardless of what religious authority, positions or titles men claim to have. You continuously choose either to obey God or men. Those not obeying Jesus are being deceived and destroyed.

Acts 20:28 in the K.J.V. that is worded as "all the flock, over the which the Holy Ghost has made you overseers" should read "in the which" or "among the which." The Greek preposition is *en* for "in" or "among" but not "over."

Only Jesus is over other persons in the Lord. Paul writes in I Tim. 2:5: "For there is one God and one mediator between God and men, the man Jesus Christ." In II Cor. 1:24, Paul states that he does not "have dominion over" the Corinthians' "faith" and "by faith you [Corinthians] stand."

I Thes. 5:12 in the K.J.V. mistranslates and speaks of men who "are over you in the lord" when it should say "who stand before you in the Lord."

II Pet. 3:2 in the K.J.V. is mistranslated to say "the commandment of us the apostles of the Lord and Savior" rather than speaking of the commandment of the Lord and Savior given you by apostles, as most other translations have it.

The statements in the K.J.V. at Rev. 1:6 and 5:10 that we are made "kings and priests to God" are ridiculous but are the result of the K.J.V. translators not having a correct manuscript from which to translate. Jesus did not make us kings and priests to

God. The right text says he made us a "kingdom, priests unto our God" or "a kingdom and priests" or a "kingdom of priests," which is what God offered the Israelites with Moses at Mt. Sinai (Ex. 19:6).

The *King James Version* and those that copied its flagrant mistranslations speak much about people ruling over others rather than serving, helping and shepherding others. We remember what Joseph told his family before they met Pharaoh: "every shepherd is an abomination unto the Egyptians" (Gen. 46:34). It seems that shepherds were also an abomination to the King James translators and they felt compelled to say that people who served others were rulers. That is a miserably sad but very serious situation.

A candidate for a bishop was to manage (literally: "stand for himself before") his own household, not "rule well his own house" as the K.J.V.'s I Tim. 3:4 has it.

Similarly, the I Tim. 5:17 K.J.V. "elders that rule well" should be: elders that do their work with diligence [literally: "stand before," Greek *proistemi*]."

Jesus says that "overcomers" will shepherd the Gentiles with a rod of iron (Rev. 2:27), not "rule" them as the K.J.V. says. And the "man child" (Rev. 12:5) and Jesus (Rev. 19:15) do not "rule the nations" as the K.J.V. says. Properly translated, the scripture says they "shepherd" the nations with a rod of iron.

The butcher drives sheep to the slaughter: the shepherd knows each sheep well, leads the sheep, cares for the sheep, protects the sheep, and finds water and pasture for them.

Peter tells the elders to lead by being "examples to the flock" and not as "lords over God's heritage" (I Pet. 5:3). Jesus said "the princes of the Gentiles exercise dominion over them; and they that are great exercise authority upon them: BUT IT SHALL NOT BE SO AMONG YOU" (Mt. 20:25,26). Jesus said "all you are brethren" and "one is your master, even Christ" (Mt. 23:8). That is how it is.

So anyone who proclaims to be a ruler of Christians is trying to usurp Jesus and hijack his church when he should be teaching men to hear, obey and live directly to Jesus and behave as Jesus behaved (I Jn. 2:6). The kidnappers are your enemies and the enemies of Christ. They impersonate God. Paul said there is "one God and one mediator [intermediary] between God and men, the man Christ Jesus" (I Tim. 2:5); and that means that no priest, pastor or "man of the cloth" is a go-between for anyone in his relating to Jesus or God. None are rulers, intermediaries, spiritual fathers, or the only men who receive revelation (Ja. 1:5-8, Mt. 7:7,8, Jn. 16:13). Jesus forbids your regarding a man as a spiritual father (Mt. 23:9). Paul was a father to the Corinthians only in that he had started their church: he "planted, Apollos watered" (I Cor. 3:6). It is deadly idolatry to regard a man as your spiritual father.

We need to say something about the so-called "fivefold ministry" of apostles, prophets, evangelists, pastors and teachers. Correctly translated (see Vincent's *Word Studies in the New Testament* or the A.S.V.), Jesus "gave some as apostles, and some as prophets, and some as evangelists, and some as pastors and teachers" (Eph. 4:11). Paul was definitely given as an apostle (I Tim. 2:7), as an evangelist (Acts 14:7), as a teacher (I Tim. 2:7), as a prophet (Gal. 1:11,12), and as a pastor with "the care of all the churches" (II Cor. 11:28). His work in Christ verified what he was. He had a calling on him and he fulfilled it. If he had not been serving Jesus carefully, he would not have had the five-fold functions that were Christ in him. He would not have been doing the authentic work as a ministry by being Jesus' voluntary slave doing what Jesus wanted him to do. His ministries were those of Eph. 4:11 that Jesus gave as gifts to the church. Paul said he was "crucified with Christ" but he lived but it was not him living but it was Christ living in him (Gal. 2:20). Without his living a crucified life and his being joined to Christ, he was nothing (I Cor. 3:6,7).

Paul was sent by God from Antioch without the say of the other apostles or any "apostolic succession." He went down to Jerusalem to check his teaching only after 14 years of establishing churches and ministering, and only because there were people coming to Antioch from the region of Jerusalem who were wrongly teaching Moses' law (Gal. 2:1-6. Acts 15:1,2). He did not claim to have a church office, position, or title other than "brother" (II Pet. 3:15). He did claim his function as an apostolic ministry, a way of serving the church. Likewise, John did not claim a position or "apostolic authority," though he did say he was old or experienced ("the elder"-III Jn. 1), when he wrote Gaius about Diotrephes (III Jn. 9,10). He did not exercise any authority over the church Gaius and Diotrephes were in.

Paul stood against Peter in Antioch when Peter was treating Gentile Christians, God's priests, as second-class members of Christ's body (Gal. 2:11,12). He said that he did not have so-called "apostolic authority" or "dominion over" the church at Corinth (II Cor. 1:24). **He said that he did not heed men because of their positions in the church** (Gal. 2:6). He did not say that he governed the church by a position he had. He did render some statements as commands in regard to people refusing to work or allowing fornication, but these were not new ordinances but were common sense and things that anyone would say in Jesus' name. They were like anyone saying: "do not kill each other."

Paul stated that he was not treated as a ruler or as many false prophets that are famous today. He said that he was a fool for Christ's sake, weak, hungry and thirsty, badly clothed, knocked about, reviled, persecuted, slandered, and despised (I Cor. 4:10-13). Christians, like Paul, should stand up for truth today and be true witnesses and undergo the unpopularity it takes to stand against delusional, dead Christianity and exciting misleading gospels and should demand that people treat Jesus as Lord and worship God in spirit and in truth.

Where the K.J.V. has Paul saying that he did "ordain" some practice, Paul actually arranged a practice or gave directions about something. He did not have power to "ordain" something; and the manuscript says he thoroughly arranged a practice (I Cor. 7:17), not that he "ordained" it.

There are a lot of false prophets (Mt. 7:15, Mt. 24:11, Mt. 24:24, II Pet. 2:1, I Jn. 4:1) and a lot of people who think they are ministries deserving honor and financial support. They destroy the kingdom of God by usurping the functions of the Holy Spirit and Christ. They do it for power over others, for money, for honor and peer approval, to unwittingly obey demons, and to bolster their egos. They often are immature but think they are above others.

The authentic church is made of ministries (servants) directed by the Holy Spirit and <u>not</u> made up of church offices or positions. An authentic person being used by Jesus **as** an apostle, prophet, evangelist, pastor or teacher will do his ministry in service to Jesus and will not make anything of himself or seek power over others. **His ministry, and all ministry, stands only by (1) the active witness and working of Jesus and by (2) the recipients'**

being able to spiritually discern his ministry as being from God (I Cor. 2:14,15).

You do not find Peter, John or Paul claiming any "apostolic authority." The only authority was God. And the only "apostolic doctrine" was just the instructions the apostles were giving in the days after the Day of Pentecost outpouring of the Holy Spirit. There was no "apostolic doctrine." The doctrinal letter to the Gentiles was advice from "the apostles, elders and brethren," not only the apostles, of what "seemed <u>good to the Holy Spirit</u> and" to them (Acts 15:23) when they came together with one accord in Christ (Acts. 15: 23-25). The advice was coming from the living Jesus among them, their being led by God.

William Branham in the middle of the 20th century attracted great crowds and was hailed as a worker of miraculous healings. He taught rubbish such as the Bible and Zodiac and pyramids being of equal spiritual value. He claimed to have a familiar spirit (demon?) named Emma leading him. He told his son to not sit in a certain chair because Emma was sitting there. He was believed by millions of deceived people, many of whom knew that he had a familiar spirit. We need to take to heart that people "perish [or "are perishing"]" "because they receive not the love of the truth that they might be saved" (II Thes. 2:10). They are following miracles and other voices than that of the Shepherd, and walking out of salvation (Heb. 5:9).

It would seem that it was stupid to follow William Branham; although (1) his ministry seemed to have power, (2) he professed to be chosen of God, (3) he drew a great following and (4) he claimed to be speaking truth.

We see such today. One was captivating many on "GOD TV" recently. He also had a familiar spirit named Emma. Because of sin, he was removed from ministry that thousands or millions were following daily; but he and Emma may be back soon.

Obvious antichrists are followed by millions. "God shall send them strong delusion" that those who do not love the truth but have pleasure in unrighteousness (religious traditions, false gospels, false prophets, false churches) will be deceived and judged (K.J.V. "damned") (II Thes. 2:11,12). Multitudes will. Those who won't give up the false and do what Jesus says will be deceived and stay in polluted churches. Satan makes people feel

81

good spiritually while they are perishing (Rev. 3:1, 3:16,17, Mt. 7:21-23).

If a person does not love the truth and is not spiritually honest, he is blocking his spiritual growth and rejecting Jesus who has come to save him from darkness. He is not coming to the light: "everyone that does evil hates the light" (Jn. 3:20). He is like a child who refuses to grow up. Sin is not doing right, not obeying God's voice (Ja. 4:17).

Many people claim to be something. Paul saw himself as what he did, his ministering and service. That was backed up by Jesus' having spoken to him and given him a "vision" of what he was to do (Acts 26:16-18) and by prophecy at Antioch (Acts 13:1-4). He did not go until he heard from Jesus. It has been said that some are called and some are sent and some just went. Paul was sure he was called and sent (Gal. 1:15,16, Rom. 1:1), "led by the Spirit" (Rom. 8:14)

Christians should have spiritual gifts imparted to them (Rom. 1:11) by "prophecy with the laying on of hands of the presbytery [**always: a number of elders**]" (I Tim. 4:14, II Tim. 1:6, I Cor. 12:4-11; Heb. 6:2). They need spiritual gifts. And They need to know the ministry God has for them (Rom. 1:11, Rom. 12:4-8; I Cor. 12:4-31, Acts 26:19, I Tim. 4:14, Acts 13:1-4, II Tim. 1:6). This often is given through a presbytery, under God's direction, who do it under a sure anointing that directs the presbytery when to pray for a person and what to prophesy. They should not pray for a person because they or the person want them to pray over him. It must be done at God's command and His time. If it is done wrong, it can cripple the recipient's life. It destroys people who think God is directing them when it is the mind of the person prophesying (and/or the Deceiver) (Rom. 1:11, Acts. 13:1-4; Acts 26:19, I Tim. 4:14). Be careful. Seek God. Regardless of your desire, do not ever be irresponsible about what **group** of elders you allow to prophesy over you about your ministry. Some get honor, status and control of others by prophesying over people: they are false prophets saying things people like to hear or what they want to say. When you know about a ministry God has given you, wait on God to use you and show you how and when to minister. It likely will not be what you like or are accustomed to or what you would choose; however, you will discover joy and God's presence when you are obeying Jesus. You will grow into a being that far exceeds anything you have hoped or thought (Eph. 3:20). You must be faithful <u>to God</u> and learn obedience to the Spirit if you are to please God and do His work. You must persevere faithfully or you will waste your life, do violence to the kingdom of God, and miss the joy God has for you.

There is an eightfold ministry listed in I Cor. 12:28 that does not mention those given to be as evangelists or pastors that are in what is called the fivefold ministry. Neither grouping has a monopoly on ministries that perfect the church.

There are multitudes of men who had rather give a man a fish every day than to teach the man to fish: they want followers after themselves and may tell you that you need to be dependent on them and attend their meetings and buy their books, tapes, anointed cloths etc. They may tell you that you cannot deal with God directly for yourself; however, if you do not deal with God for yourself, you are into idolatry and deceived. Those who sell books, tapes and prayer cloths are making God's house not "a house of prayer" (Mt. 21:13) but a house or merchandize or a "den of thieves" (Mt. 21:13). They want honor and money. They are like those who extort tithes. No one should make a profit from what God gives them but should "freely give" as they have "freely" "received" (Mt. 10:8). If this book, for instance, should make a profit, it should **not** go to the writer. A man should not take money for ministry God gives him. Also, a man should not receive honor from men for his faithfulness to God or for ministry God gives him.

Though in the last of the first century there came to be in some churches the creation of both man-ordained priests and laymen, the separation of Christians into men over men is an abomination to God and to Christ who personally is in each and directing each "born again" Christian. There came to be the beliefs that certain men themselves were holy and others were not. Buildings were thought to be holy when there first began to be church buildings in the early 4th century under Constantine's influence; and they often still are. Some buildings were thought to be holy only because of relics that were kept in chests. A chair or *cathedra* (from which we get *cathedral*) was considered to be holy. There came to be a holy section of a church building where only men called priests could go. There had not been any church buildings before the first part of the fourth century; churches had met in homes, catacombs, grave yards and other places. Priest costumes and colored church house windows and soothing music came into vogue. Chairs for the members, a pulpit and the idea of a congregation facing a man in a pulpit came into use instead of the earlier practice of all participants standing or sitting in a circle with no pulpit. High ceilings and steeples were added.

Tithing had not existed in the early church for about 200 years until Cyprian, a bishop at Alexandria, got it started in Alexandria as a tax to be used to support the poor and help some deacons and bishops. It was not widespread in the 3rd century but increased in the 4th century when it provided more revenue than the clergy salaries paid by Constantine.

Tithing was not required or suggested by "the apostles and elders and brethren" in Jerusalem. They sent a letter to Gentile churches telling them which religious laws that it seemed good to them and to the Holy Ghost to require of the Gentiles. Gentile Christians were only to "abstain from meats offered to idols, and from blood, and from things strangled, and from fornication [N.T. "fornication" is any kind of sexual sin including adultery]" (Acts 15:23,28,29). They were not told to tithe; nor are we told to do so.

If Jesus owns a man, he owns all that he has such that tithing, 10%, is much less of what is required of a man than is one's living to Jesus 100%. Tithing today would be robbing God of your wholly being His servant. Tithing is not mentioned in the New Testament as being done by any Christian. Christians are "not under the law" (Rom. 6:14, Gal. 5:18) and tithing is from the law. If a Christian is "justified by the law," he is "fallen from grace" (Gal. 5:4).

Abraham once gave a tenth of some war spoils to Melchisedec (Gen. 14:18-20, Heb. 7:1,2). Some people think that that was because God required tithing before Moses' law was given. Actually, Abraham had come from Mesopotamia where pagan gods were given one tenth of the spoils of war. Tithing to various gods was widespread among many of the pagan peoples in Abraham's time. Jacob, who may have been copying his grandfather Abraham, made an offer to give God a tithe of his collected belongings if God kept him and returned him safely from

84

Haran (Gen. 28:20-22). However, there was never any biblical regular tithing practiced by God's people except for what was under the law of Moses. Jesus said that the Jews under the law of Moses should have tithed (Mt. 23:23) and God said the Jews under the law of Moses had robbed Him by not tithing (Mal. 3:8). Now you can rob God by tithing.

People who called themselves priests first began extorting tithes from men, as we said above, about A.D. 230; and greed fueled tithing after the first of the 4th century.

Tithing was not done in the earlier church. It is kept alive by ignorance. People are being extorted by churches that require their people to tithe and by those who make false statements about the benefits of tithing and penalties for not tithing. It teaches men should not put all they have at God's disposal, "on the altar." It is law and deadly anti-Christian.

To some, it teaches you can obtain money by giving to a ministry. Television ministries parade success stories of people who say they have become rich because they started tithing. **They use fear and intimidate people by claiming financial disaster will befall anyone who does not tithe**.

And what was and is the trouble that allowed and is allowing the mass destruction to the real church? It was and is that the participants were and are not "born again" sheep living to their Shepherd and being led by the Spirit and **hearing and obeying God's voice**, the voice of the Shepherd He sent. Jesus is being kept out of the church.

Men were and are doing and teaching convenient nonsense from their own minds. They honor each other and not God (Jn. 5:44). They are hearing and obeying men and their traditions and not following the Shepherd and seeing to it that Jesus is their Lord and Shepherd. Where churches were or are not spiritual, they must be run by men like a business is run. And we see "churches" everywhere now that are not the living body of Christ by any stretch of the imagination. Each calls itself a church but well may be what Jesus would call a "synagogue of Satan" (Rev. 2:9, 3:9), **an imposter keeping men from God's kingdom**.

The Catholic Church was burning Bibles even in the 20th Century. They were adamant in the 1500's and later that the scriptures, God's words to His people, should not be in a language that most of their people could read. One of their ruling leaders had never read a verse in the Bible.

The baptism that Jesus brought to give us power to participate with God is the baptism in the Holy Ghost. It was only a memory among most churches 140 years after it was first poured out. It again was almost unknown in the United States until about A.D. 1900 and then the Azusa Street outpouring in 1906. It is still unknown to many. Authentic Christians are being robbed of their citizenship in God and His kingdom by (1) the churches that spew out false teachings, (2) corrupt men controlling and ruling the weak, and (3) churches opposing the kingdom of God.

Paul said that "the time" would "come when" men ("Christians") would "not endure sound doctrine: but after their own lusts shall they heap up to themselves teachers…and they shall turn away their ears from the truth, and shall be turned unto fables." (II Tim. 4:3,4). That time has come and been here, and that is what this book is about. It is about our becoming outraged and about our now decontaminating ourselves from fables and about engaging ourselves only in truth, God, Christ and God's kingdom.

Jesus likened the kingdom of heaven to "a grain of mustard seed which a man took and cast into his garden, and it grew and waxed a great tree; and the fowls of the air lodged in the branches of it" (Lk. 13:18,19). The place Christ should rule became not a four-foot tall plant, but a great tree. Jesus had planted the word, and it became polluted with something different from what Jesus planted because of Satan's work in it. It had birds living in it that were not part of the tree, not part of the kingdom of God.

That is what we see today: many preachers that are not part of the church but are living on it and the church becoming glorious in man's eyes but being something different from the lowly, despised body of Christ. We see the blind leading the blind. That is the "tares" in the field, the wicked ones sewn by the devil (Mt. 13:38,39) that are appearing as angels [messengers] of light (II Cor. 11:14).

You cannot know what a church of Spirit-led, truth-hungry, Christ-manifesting, obedient participants in Christ and his love will normally experience unless you have tasted of the unhindered moving of Christ in such an assembly. Real churches do not need special music, a choir, hired preachers, men ruling men or following men, steeples, a special building, church clothes, painted windows, shouting preachers, leaders not from the local church, only one man preaching in a meeting, pews, vestments, programs, public address systems that damage your ears, arrogance, respect of persons, tithing, or a mass of other poisons. Members need to be Spirit baptized and individually living by hearing the VOICE of the Shepherd and obediently following the Shepherd. And all need to be listening to one another in whom Jesus dwells, "submitting yourselves one to another in the fear of God" (Eph. 5:21). Their meetings need to be characterized by the anointing of God that sometimes is so strong that it transfixes you. It comes when 2 or 3 or more are gathered in Jesus' name (Mt. 18:20), are fully listening to and obeying Christ and refraining from doing anything routine or anything God is not directing. Meeting locations are mostly unimportant.

Paul spoke of the church being "built upon the foundation of the apostles and the prophets, Jesus Christ himself being the chief corner stone" (Eph. 2:20). The apostles to whom Paul referred were likely those to whom Peter referred. They were those that continually "companied with" them "all the time that the Lord Jesus went in and out among" them "beginning from the baptism of John, unto that same day that he was taken up" (Acts 1:21,22). They were necessary to be witnesses "of his [Jesus'] resurrection" (Acts 1:22). Peter went to Cornelius' house and said that he was a witness "of all things which he [Jesus] did," and was then a witness that God raised Jesus from the dead. He said that God showed Jesus openly to witnesses that God had chosen beforehand and who ate and drank with Jesus after he rose from the dead. He said that Jesus commanded the witnesses to preach and testify that he is made judge of the living (us) and the dead (Acts 10:39-42). These witnesses and their gospels and letters are vital church foundations.

However, there are modern teachings that present day apostles themselves (not even both "apostles and prophets" as in Eph. 2:20) must be the foundation of the church now. And that is the same old church destroying idolatry that Jesus has set men over men such that God has other intermediaries than Jesus between Himself and men. Only churches that are spiritually bankrupt need hierarchies with men usurping God and requiring obedience to themselves.

Ancient and present prophets are vital to the church. Their prophecies must be judged by individuals. The Holy Spirit is the Spirit of truth. "The natural man receives not the things of the Spirit of God: for they are foolishness unto him, neither can he know them because they are spiritually discerned. But he that is spiritual judges all things…" (I Cor. 2:14,15). We must be made spiritual to know the truth. A person who continues hearing and **doing** Jesus' word will be knowing the truth (Jn. 8:31,32). To be spiritual we have to wait on the Spirit as He renews and inhabits our minds. A spiritually minded person will not follow a stranger. He listens and waits for the Shepherd's voice. The church operates only as it hears Jesus. Neither signs and wonders nor a person's claims about himself authenticate a man.

Apostles were the 12 appointed by Jesus, Matthias who replaced Judas, Paul and Barnabas, and maybe 7 or more people including Silas and Timothy. The 12 that included Matthias were with Jesus for about three years. Jesus taught the eleven about the kingdom for 40 days after he arose.

The word *apostle* means "one sent forth." Paul was sent forth; however Paul was not a witness of all Jesus did and said. Jesus did appear to Paul as he has to many of us. The 12 witnessed and verified Jesus' resurrection and what Jesus said and did; and they wrote letters and Gospels.

We know that Paul had "the care [but not control] of all the churches" (II Cor. 11:28), began churches, traveled among the churches, wrote letters, expounded doctrine and Jesus' revelation to him, worked with traveling assistants and administered miracles. He prophesied ministries and imparted spiritual gifts. Peter said he was an elder writing to Christians in general and also addressing the elders among them (I Pet. 5:1-4). We know that Peter traveled among churches, made a visit to Antioch with their Gentile Christians, performed miracles, wrote some letters to churches, raised a dead woman, was sent to Cornelius' house, ministered the baptism in the Holy Spirit to Samaritans to whom Philip ministered, and preached the gospel in Samaritan villages. He was very active in Jerusalem after the outpouring of the Holy Spirit and was a leader there before Rome demolished Jerusalem in A.D. 70.

John traveled to churches, wrote letters and a Gospel and was a leader in Jerusalem along with Peter and James, Jesus' brother. He, with Peter, ministered to the Samaritans.

Present day Christians may be sent forth by Jesus: however they should not be heeded because of who they say they are or just because of signs and wonders. God will let Satan have "power and signs and lying wonders" (II Thes. 2:9); and "false Christs and false prophets" now show "great signs and wonders" to deceive (Mt. 24:24). We must look for spiritual fruits that are not artificial and "prove all things" and "test the spirits" and not put our confidence in man. We will see a lot better when we make sure that we all are seeking to have Jesus be the leader of each of our lives and of the church and we refuse to accept anything but our hearing the Shepherd's voice and following where he leads. Jesus causes men to "speak as the oracles of God," but many false teachers say they are speaking for God. Every kind of false prophet appeared in the first century: they appear today wherever they find gullible men.

An assembly that is too large would prevent people from knowing and loving one another as Christ loved us and would prevent each member from exercising his gifts and ministry. It might be that an assembly with over about 100 members would be led to split and form 2 assemblies. It is necessary for all to be listening to Jesus and ministering.

Pews and a pulpit can prevent authentic worship meetings. Large numbers of participants can prevent the interaction of ministries that should characterize a church meeting. Every member needs to be and know that he or she is an effective priest or priestess who is knowing and doing God's will.

It is absolutely necessary and possible to have all Spirit-baptized servants of Jesus participating in meetings and in the ministry of the church to itself and to be doing the will of Christ in the meetings and in all their lives. God may be speaking through even a 7 year-old child. God may completely turn a life upside down by a remark from a person who does not even know he is being used. When God anoints a meeting, a person often can know beyond a shadow of doubt what God is saying. Living by what God and the Shepherd are saying is living "by faith, not by sight" (II Cor. 5:7). Anointed Church meetings can and should be the happiest and most meaningful experiences a person has ever had. "Where the Spirit of the Lord is, there is liberty" (II Cor. 3:17). We need to be church and let Jesus into his church.

Where a meeting is not anointed, people should go home. There is no point in meeting when Christ is not actively present. He will be there ministering where 2 or 3 or more are gathered in his name, in his character. People should come to a meeting having waited on Jesus. We should not expect him where people are not reverencing him.

Members cannot plan an authentic meeting. Rather, they must be led by the Spirit in their waiting on God and having Him leading and preparing them such that each can minister "a psalm" (anointed song that could be a new song never heard before of after), "a doctrine" (teaching), "a revelation" (from God), "a tongue" (anointed unknown language), or "an interpretation" (I Cor. 14:26) and is anointed to prophesy. Who, when, and how ministries will be used will not be known until the Holy Spirit weaves the meeting together into a glorious ministry. The leader is Jesus speaking through the Holy Spirit. It is always awesome. It is the functioning of Christ's body. It is likely the reason Paul said "if Christ be not raised, your faith is vain [only delusion]" (I Cor. 15:17), because Christ could not be leading or living in us if he were not raised.

What is difficult is our dealing with those who want to take over and set themselves in control of others or monopolize ministry. They can prevent Jesus' ministry. They can be sophomores (sophisticated morons), heretical teachers, immature brethren who are "weak in the faith" (Rom. 14:1), the deceived children of "the wicked one" (Mt. 13:38), or men drawing "away disciples after them" and wanting "the preeminence" (Acts 20:30, III Jn. 9).

Members must submit to God and "one to another in the fear of God" (Eph. 5:21). Each must "try [be testing] the spirits whether they are of God" (I Jn. 4:1) and "prove [be testing] all things: hold fast that which is good [or right]" (I Thes. 5:21). Jesus' "sheep" "hear his voice" and he "goes before them, and the sheep follow him, for they know his voice; and a stranger will they not follow, but will flee from him, for they know not the voice of strangers" (Jn. 10:3-5). Recognizing and fleeing from spiritual strangers' voices should function in Christian life.

Because there are many who are bewitched by false prophets, false teachings, false brethren, false translations, false churches, "the commandments of men" (Mt. 15:9), their being "puffed up" (I Cor. 4:6,18), the need to be honored by men (Jn. 5:44, Rom. 2:29), the love of money (I Tim. 6:10), and other carnality (I Cor. 3:3), Christians are often abused. They have to be "wise as serpents and harmless as doves" (Mt. 10:16), aware of a person's "fruits" (Mt. 7:16,20), testing all things (I Thes. 5:21), and trying the spirits whether they are of God (I Jn. 4:1). Paul spoke of his being reviled, persecuted, defamed, and considered "the filth of the world" (I Cor. 4:12,13).

Jesus tells his people to get out of the false church so they will not be partners in her sins (Rev. 18:4).

The authentic body of Jesus is nothing like the "virus" contaminated, "worm" infested church order that many think is the real church. Those who love the truth should not fellowship where Jesus is being ignored and disrespected and men are making names for themselves and their organizations and "make merchandise of" men (II Pet. 2:3, Rev. 18:11-13). Each Christian is a priest of God and has or has assigned to him a unique ministry that is Christ's working in and through him. He needs to avoid the phony church like the plague and live where he can hear God for himself and participate in Jesus.

The genuine church is composed of people who help one another live to Jesus. The enticing phony church enslaves people to live to itself.

7

God's Plan

God tells us a little about His plan. We will look at some of it.

God said: "let us make man in our image, after our likeness: and let them have dominion over the fish of the sea, and over the fowl of the air, and over the cattle and over all the earth, and over every creeping thing that creeps upon the earth" (Gen. 1:26). Gen. 1:27 says: "so God created man in His own image." David wrote: "What is man that You are mindful of him? And the son of man that You visit him? For You have made him a little lower than the angels and have crowned him with glory and honor. You made him to have dominion over the works of Your hands: You have put all things under his feet..." (Ps. 8:4-6).

Has this happened? Yes, but only to Jesus as far as we know. Jesus, after his resurrection, came and said: "All power is given unto me in heaven and in earth" (Mt. 28:18). Heb. 2:8,9 refers to Ps. 8 and says: "You have put all things in subjection under his [man's] feet. For in that He put all in subjection under him [under men], He left nothing that is not put under him [men]. But now we see not yet all things put under him. But we see Jesus... crowned with glory and honor." Jesus has fulfilled Gen. 1:26,27, Ps. 8:4-6, and Heb. 2:8,9.

What is going on? The answer is in the ancient Hebrew language. The language had no future perfect tense. It had only something like a present tense and something like a past tense and a way of indicating the future. The imprecise Hebrew verb can be translated: "I will have made man in My likeness" and "all things will be under him with him being crowned with honor and glory." It is a sure thing that that is how it will be for us. But Heb. 2:8,9 says only that it has come for Jesus. We should desire, fight for, seek and expect it. We should "war a good warfare" (I Tim. 1:18), overcome (Rev. 3:21), have "fought a good fight...kept the faith" (II Tim. 4:7), and "run with patience the race... set before us" (Heb. 12:1).

The fact is that man is not in God's image yet, not over all the works of God's hands, and not crowned with glory and honor. Only Jesus is. The rest of us have a ways to go.

If God had already made man in His image, then there would never have been the need for men to be "changed into the same image [Jesus' and God's] from glory to glory [not be completely changed all at once in a "revival" service]" "by the Spirit of the Lord" (II Cor. 3:18). They would not have needed to be "transformed [go through metamorphosis] by the renewing of" their minds (Rom. 12:2) and overcome (Rev. 3:21,Gen. 4.7) and suffer with Jesus (Rom. 8:17). Jesus, who was sinless, had to mature and be made perfect by sufferings (Heb. 2:10), learn obedience by the things which he suffered (Heb. 5:8), grow mentally and emotionally (Lk. 2:52), overcome (Rev. 3:21), and love good and hate evil (Isa. 7:15). Will not we who were shaped in iniquity need to do the same, and not because we have sinned but because any living soul must, like Jesus, learn, grow, choose good and become faithful?

It is spiritual suicide to not be knowing that we are being made into Jesus' and God's image exactly as God has always intended. It is spiritual suicide to not know that we are learning to be smart and choose good and hate evil and that that takes experience and may cost us everything the same as it did for Jesus our "forerunner" (Heb. 6:20) and pioneer (Heb. 2:10) and example (I Pet. 2:21) whom we follow. Jesus said: "he that loses his life for my sake shall find it" (Mt. 10:39) and "fear not them which kill the body, but are not able to kill the soul" (Mt. 10:28).

Paul tells us that the "first man Adam was made a living soul" and was "natural" and "earthy" and that the "last Adam" or "second man" "who is the Lord from heaven" was made a "quickening [life-giving] spirit" and was spiritual. He then tells us that "as we have borne the image of the earthy, we shall also bear the image of the heavenly" (I Cor. 15:45-49). Paul, like Hebrews 2:8,9, is saying that no **men except Jesus have ever been in the image of God** but we will be in His image as Jesus is now. Jesus had to "overcome" (Rev. 3.21) and be made "perfect through sufferings" (Heb. 2:10, 5:8). Will not we need to do so?

That is foundational fact. Man did not "fall." Adam started in innocence like a baby who knows nothing of good and

94

evil, good and bad. Adam was not spiritual and did not "fall" from God's plan, love or grace. To grow up morally, children need training and supervised freedom to choose. To grow up spiritually, they need the same. Adam had to learn, Jesus had to learn, and we have to learn. You do not get experience without experience: and experience is necessary in the formation of character.

Paul says we begin as "natural," "earthy," "living souls" which is what the animals were made (I Cor. 15:45-47). However, men are destined to be over all the works of God's hands. Men, you and I, are to be "joint-heirs" with Christ **if** we suffer with him (Rom. 8:17). We are to sit with him in his throne **if** we overcome as he did (Rev. 3:21).

Jesus is "the <u>image</u> of... God" (Col. 1:15), "the... <u>image</u> of His person" (Heb. 1:3), "the <u>image</u> of God" (II Cor. 4:4).

"But we all...beholding as in a glass [looking glass or mirror] the glory of the Lord, are changed [undergo metamorphosis] into the same <u>image</u> from glory to glory even as by the Spirit of the Lord" (II Cor. 3:18). We "shall also bear the <u>image</u> of the heavenly" Adam (I Cor. 15:49), "the Lord from heaven." God's Son became "the firstborn among many brethren [men becoming into the image of God-Rom. 8:29]." He, Jesus, became and is "the <u>man</u> Christ Jesus" (I Tim. 2:5). "Whom He [God] did foreknow [us], He also did predestinate to be conformed to the <u>image</u> of His Son" (Rom. 8:29). Jesus' "brethren" (Rom. 8:29, Jn. 20:17) are to be "transformed [undergo metamorphosis] by the renewing of" their "mind" (Rom. 12:2). God carries us through changes, metamorphosis, as we press into His kingdom, His living in us and guiding us.

In short, we are to become and are becoming in the image of Jesus which is the image of God. We will be in the image of Jesus who is the image of God after we undergo the metamorphosis or transformation to be in that image. And that should be our goal: to be like Jesus (I Jn. 3:2). Paul wholeheartedly pressed "toward the mark for the prize of the high calling of God in Christ Jesus" (Phil. 3:14).

Mankind made a beginning of becoming like God when Eve was deceived by the "serpent" that was "more subtle than any beast of the field which the Lord God had made" (Gen. 3:1). Her eyes and then the eyes of Adam, who also ate of the fruit of the

Tree of the Knowledge of Good and Evil, were opened to know good and bad, good and evil (Gen. 3:1-7). God let the subtlest beast into His nursery to fool Eve and to cause Adam and Eve to see good and bad.

God was pleased, not upset, angry or disappointed. He had prepared "the Lamb slain from the foundation of the world" (Rev. 13:8). He did not destroy Adam and Eve or cause them to be barren. He was going to make billions more like them: natural, earthy, living souls. That is how men **must be** before they undergo metamorphosis into being spiritual. They must go through experience: "by reason of use have their senses exercised to discern both good and evil" (Heb. 5:14). Character comes as we make difficult and self-sacrificial right choices.

They had come to know themselves as being naked. They lived for themselves, selfishly; and a person's selfish carnality is not what the person wants to be seen. It is unacceptable. Men use manners or politeness to conceal or clothe their selfishness. Manners do not make them righteous. They cover up or clothe their carnality. Religious legalism, like politeness and social manners, is a cover and control for carnality. Peter said that "neither our fathers nor we were able to bear" the legalism (Acts 15:10). Many now try to cover their carnality by claiming that they are right with God because Jesus died in their place. John straightened out such foolishness: "let no man deceive you: he that does righteousness is righteous, even as he [Jesus] is righteous" (I Jn. 3:7). Righteousness is by faithfulness that produces right acts and not by dead faith (Ja. 2:17,20).

Jesus said that the church at Laodicea was naked (Rev. 3:17) and needed to "buy" or do what it takes to get the "white raiment" that the overcomers will receive (Rev. 3:5) and is akin to the "white" "linen" that is the "righteousness of the saints" (Rev. 19:8). We say this because it is necessary that we come through experience to know that nakedness that needs to hide is our lot until we repent and die to our old selves and become obedient parts of God who is love and unselfishness which is righteous clothing that we want as clothing. Our motives, "the thoughts and intents of the heart" (Heb. 4:12), need to be changed. Jesus does not just clothe carnality; he replaces it with clothing that is God's life, God Himself, the life of the Eternal that does not need to hide or be ashamed. It is love, wholly goodness, righteousness, life, truth, patience, knowledge, spiritual light, wisdom, faith and much more.

God said; "Behold, the man is become **as one of us** to know good and evil" (Gen. 3:22). Man did not fall. He had become **more like God** and was on his way to becoming fully in the likeness of God. If men had not had their eyes opened to know good and evil, to be involved in good and evil, they would not have ever become in the image (likeness) of God Who knows good and evil. It takes experience and wisdom to make character that will die for the truth and choose good over evil. We learn to live from good motives and refuse the stupidity of selfishness.

Now men would need, like Jesus their example, to learn "to refuse the evil and choose the good" (Isa. 7:15) and to have "loved righteousness and hated iniquity" (Heb. 1:9). They have to "by reason of use have their senses exercised to discern both good and evil" (Heb. 5:14): they have to have their spiritual eyes trained by **experience** to know what is good and what is bad and to "not henceforth live unto themselves, but unto" Jesus (II Cor. 5:15).

You only understand good and evil when you value good enough to live or die for it and you live to do good. It happens through experience and gives you wisdom. It is a life-challenging, 24/7 venture. It might be that God has you be unrecognized for your service in taking care of an Alzheimer victim and you lose much of your life in doing so. It might be that you become a laughing stock for standing up for the truth or for people who cannot stand up for themselves. It might be that you need to trust what God has said to you when everyone tells you that you are a fool. Discerning good and evil is life and is not for the timid; and many people do not want that vital responsibility. It requires action and will cost you everything and make you a different and truly spiritual person. God told Cain that he must overcome sin, "rule over" it (Gen. 4:7).

Men are introduced to this world with consciences that can tell them when they do wrong, but only if and when they know what is right. They also have many urges to do wrong. Their hearts, when they are not controlled by them and by God, as had been righteous Abel's heart, are "deceitful above all things and desperately wicked" (Jer. 17:9).

They are born with a BIG problem: knowing and doing good and hating evil. Doing evil is easy and often fun. Even a dead fish can swim downstream. Doing good gets you persecution and rejection from friends, family, and authorities and will cost you everything and make you a faithful and free son of God. Men face temptations and make decisions about good and evil every time they do or say anything. But they enter this world unprepared to make good choices, ignorant of their needs, selfishly driven and needing to continually learn and grow in **wisdom**, as Jesus did (Lk. 2:52). God made it that way. A philosopher said cynically: "and on the seventh day, God snickered."

Actually, God makes our circumstances so that we will seek, find (Acts 17:27), value and participate in Him. We may feel that it is unfair, but we are born with a need and responsibility to overcome and control our natural natures in which we were born as well as many physical and psychological shortcomings and the wrong thinking the world and role models teach us from birth on. All of these are not of our making. They are given to us by God: and our overcoming them will make us God's sons in Jesus' image, mature spiritual souls.

Men are not born at all experienced with choosing good and bad; and they are easily deceived as was Eve and as are multitudes of deceived "Christians." Cain brought a wrong offering to God. God said that he would not be accepted by Him if sin was lying at the door and that sin would want to rule him but he must rule sin, that he had the responsibility to do his part to be righteous, to overcome doing wrong and to do good and do what is right (Gen. 4:7).

Sin causes death to a living relationship with God who is righteous and is love, (Isa. 59:2, I Jn. 4:8,16, Dan. 9:14) and it destroys men being subject to God (Rom. 8:7). It turns men over to error, being led by their natural minds directed by their bodies and egos which are not subject to God (Rom. 8:7, Eph. 2:3). Men do themselves harm and cause themselves confusion while they are believing they are doing well. But they are deceived and shortsighted and do not know what "well" is. They do not know God's plan for them. Doing "well" is undergoing metamorphosis into the spiritual and mental image or likeness of God and into knowledge of God at any cost. It is God's getting His fingerprints

98

in you and changing you from glory to glory into Jesus' likeness. It is being in union with God such that God lives in you and is your life. "God so loved the world that he gave his only begotten son that whosoever" is being faithful to, trusting and obeying him, should not be being destroyed but should be having everlasting life [life of the Everlasting God] (Jn. 3:16). In other words, we really do need a savior to save us from our being stupid and destroying ourselves. We need to participate in Jesus and God's kingdom and allow Jesus (his "blood" or soul) to cleanse us "from all sin [all error, failure or rebellion]" (I Jn. 1:7) and give us a new life of service and love for others in obedience to our Shepherd.

Men are "shaped in iniquity" (Ps. 51:5). They learn from parents and friends who often teach them that evils such as selfishness, hatred, bigotry, lying, fornication, gossip, abortion, loving wealth, judging others etc. are good. Before they can reason, they model after men who are their examples and role models who are not like Jesus and who commit wrong in deed and word; and their undeveloped minds are warped. Their minds are undeveloped and going through challenges for which they have no preparation, and they may be under stress at home and elsewhere such that they cannot think and make good decisions. They may be abused and have anger and distrust in them that is not of their making. They may not have any good role models or righteous associates. They sometimes use their simple minds to deal with complex situations; and they think that they are sufficient to understand things without experience and without God. Still, God helps and protects them.

They grow in stature and become clumsy until their brains learn to compensate for their new dimensions. Puberty thrusts them into a need to make choices for which they are not ready. They have false fears that cause them to be more interested in self-preservation and in prestige among men than in right living. They have desires from their flesh that they must rule or they will be ruled by their desires. They think that they will miss out on things they need if they are honest and do what is right. They are mostly unaware that they live in God (Acts 17:28) or that there is God. They form strong dependencies on the approval and opinions of their peers and of authorities who often misdirect, take advantage of and misuse them. They do four things wrong when they try to do one thing right. In many ways they are "shaped in iniquity" (Ps. 51:5) and need to be rescued from perishing to having everlasting life, (Jn. 3:16), God's life.

They need a savior, a reliable right EXAMPLE. Jesus in the Revelation is first called "the faithful witness" (Rev. 1:5). He was Immanuel, God with us. He said: "I am...the truth" (Jn. 14:6). He is our "EXAMPLE" (I Pet. 2:21) and "forerunner" (Heb. 6:20) and is our "captain [trailblazer]" (Heb. 2:10), God's faithful son. Jesus said the reason he was "born" and "came" "into the world" was "to bear witness unto the truth" (Jn. 18:37).

When a child injures a father who is abusing his mother, he thinks he is doing something good. When one first takes a narcotic, he believes he is doing something good. When he tells a lie, he is doing great damage to his ability to know what is true; and he thinks he is in control when he is becoming insensitive to truth much like a drunk who thinks he is getting better as he drinks himself irresponsible.

Some grow up believing that murder, abusing, lying, violence, fornication, betrayal, disloyalty, and selfishness are virtues to be cultivated. The government of the United States has refused repeatedly to make a law to stop partial birth abortion, the murder of healthy babies as they are coming out of a mother's womb at birth. The government approves murder and then wonders why its citizens murder. The states that once regarded fornication and adultery as being punishable by law, are now regarding the two as acceptable behavior. Politicians lie and get proven to be lying by videotape evidence shown on TV, and then get important positions in government. Schools teach science fiction as fact and outlaw truth and facts. They teach immorality is just an acceptable lifestyle. Such is the iniquity on every side in which men are shaped and from which they need an escape (Ps. 51:5). They need a living savior and shepherd.

So men are born into a world that gives them wrong understandings and bad examples of right and wrong; and each person has a conscience that needs to believe he is doing right. They have many pressures to lie and to become hardened; and they have great peer pressure to just do what others do. They often have little pressure on them to do what is right or to even know what is right. They commit wrong and reprogram their souls to believe that wrong acts are necessary and therefore are good. That is what the "should not perish [be perishing]" in Jn. 3:16 is about.

Sin is not about God being offended or about His not allowing us into Heaven some day: it is about men self-destructing by damaging the integrity of their souls and becoming souls that in their condition cannot be part of God and prosper. Men become foolish and get disabled to be choosing good. Solomon says we should get wisdom or we will self-destruct, perish (Pro. 1:20-33). "The fear of the Lord is the beginning of wisdom" (Psa. 111:10).

God has a program. Jesus has gone through it first. Jesus is the "captain of" our "salvation" (Heb. 2:10); or more correctly translated, Jesus is the person to go a way first, the trail blazer or pioneer who will be followed by people doing what he has done. The K.J.V. "captain" is translated in other translations as "leader" and "pioneer."

If we "believe in him" (Jn. 3:16) in the sense that a correct translation says we must, then we avail ourselves of him, obey him, trust him, believe him and put our dependence on him. That is how we get "everlasting life," divine life that is not subject to death and decay. We get everlasting life by abiding in Jesus, which is what the "believing in him" means (Jn. 15:1-6). We follow his "example" (I Pet 2:21). Then "the blood of Jesus Christ [the life or soul of Jesus-see pages 38 and 42]" is cleansing "us from all sin" (I Jn. 1:7): sin is error, failure or rebellion. Jesus then will "deliver us from this present evil world" for which Jesus "gave himself" for us (Gal. 1:4). Jesus "suffered for sins" "that he might bring us to God" (I Pet. 3:18). Jesus then is the "author of eternal salvation unto all them who obey him" (Heb. 5:9), which is, again, to "believe in him" of Jn. 3:16 and abide in him and in the kingdom of God and the New Covenant. That is salvation; and the phony gospel is delusion that keeps men from the gospel of the kingdom of God and real salvation and teaches them live in fear of and separated from an ungodly god rather than being God's priests and kingdom. Like the animal sacrifices made under Moses' law, the phony gospel only makes "remembrance" of "sins" (Heb. 10:3): it does nothing to "save men" "from their sins" as does the living Jesus (Mt. 1:21, Eph. 2:5).

101

Jesus "made himself of no reputation [literally: he emptied himself of what he had been], and took upon him the form of a servant, and was made in the likeness of men" (Phil. 2:7). Jesus came from above but was "made" or transformed into being just a man. "In ALL THINGS it behooved him to be made like unto his brethren [a man, fully man]" (Heb. 2:17). Jesus "was in ALL POINTS tempted like as we are" (Heb. 4:15). "He" "learned" "obedience by the things which he suffered" (Heb. 5:8). He was made "perfect through sufferings" (Heb. 2:10).

Jesus "suffered for us, leaving us an **example**, that" we "should follow his steps [his example]" (I Pet. 2:21). As we have quoted, he "suffered for sins" "that he might bring us to God" (I Pet. 3:18) and he "gave himself for our sins that he might deliver us from this present evil world" (Gal. 1:4). He demonstrated living to God, being a son to God and growing and being changed to be in God's image.

Jesus gave up his divine place and relationship with God and was transformed to be a man. As a man, he overcame everything that men face (Heb. 4:15) while having only the supernatural powers that are available to other men. He became wholly in God's likeness and entered fully into God as a spiritual man and quickening (life giving) spirit (Heb. 6:20, I Tim. 2:5, I Cor. 15:45), now a man in the image of God crowned with honor and glory and having dominion over the creation. He did not sin (Heb. 4:15); he obeyed God and was "made perfect" (Heb. 2:10, Heb. 5:9). He became "the firstborn among many brethren" (Rom. 8:29), men "conformed to the image of" God's "Son" (Rom. 8:29). It is by virtue of his being made "perfect through sufferings" (Heb. 2:10) and that he "overcame" that he "set down with" his "Father" "in His throne" (Rev. 3:21). He "loved righteousness and hated iniquity" (Heb. 1:9) and qualified to be given "all power" "in heaven and in earth" (Mt. 28:18, I Cor. 15:27). If Jesus had not been faithful and overcome temptations and abuse by men, he would not be sitting in his Father's throne and be ruling. He underwent the suffering that was necessary for him to be made perfect. He had to be made to have a heart that was faithful to God and that did God's will ("learned" "obedience by the things which he suffered" – Heb. 5:8). As a man he attained to be worthy of and later to receive the divine glory and interaction with God that he had had (Jn.17:5) and gave up when he emptied himself of divinity (p. 102) to become a man "in ALL THINGS" "made like unto his brethren" (Heb. 2:17, Phil. 2:7). He did what we must do. He said: "To him that overcomes will I grant to sit with me in my throne, even as I also overcame and am set down with my Father in His throne" (Rev. 3:21). Jesus is crowned with glory and honor and is set over the works of God's hands. He now forever continues to be our brother, "the MAN Christ Jesus" (I Tim. 2:5).

Jesus said: "Except a corn of wheat fall into the ground and die, it abides alone; but if it die it brings forth much fruit" (Jn. 12:24). Jesus is bringing forth us as "much fruit," seeds that are like the seed Jesus that fell into the ground.

Being God's only begotten is not what qualified Jesus. His obedience even "unto death, even the death of the cross" (Phil. 2:8), his voluntary suffering, that he "loved righteousness and hated iniquity" (Heb. 1:9), his overcoming, and his being made perfect into the image of God so that "in him dwells all the fullness of the Godhead bodily" (Col. 2:9), made him the dwelling place of God and "our forerunner" entered into the holiest place (Heb. 6:20).

Jesus has done it. He is the pioneer (K.J.V. "captain") of our salvation (Heb. 2:10), the first man to go from being a living soul to being "made" a life-giving spirit, a spiritual man in God's image whose image we will bear (I Cor. 15: 45-49; Rom. 8:29; II Cor. 3:18). As a few men have gone by rockets into space and escaped the gravity of the earth, Jesus overcame the gravity of carnality controlling him and became our "forerunner" (Heb. 6:20) entered fully into God.

Now we "ought" "also to walk [live and behave] even as he walked [lived]" (I Jn. 2:6). We, who are baptized in the Holy Spirit, can do that because we through the Holy Spirit have the assets and opportunity he had.

"If so be that we suffer with" Jesus, we will be "joint-heirs with Christ" (Rom. 8:17). Jesus is the "firstborn among many brethren" (Rom. 8:29), and we are invited to be his next-born brethren who are those who "do the will of God [are doing the will of God]" (Mt. 12:50, Mk. 3:35) and "hear the word of God and do it [are hearing and doing God's word]" (Lk. 8:21) and overcome (Rev. 2:7, 2:11, 2:17, 2:26, 3:5, 3:12, 3:21).

Briefly stated, Jesus put off his divine self (Phil. 2:7-"emptied himself"-A.S.V.) and became a man (Phil. 2:7,8, I Tim. 2:5). He was made "in all things" to be like us "his brethren" (Heb. 2:17). He grew mentally: "increased in wisdom and stature, and in favor with God and with man" (Lk. 2:52). He was made "perfect through sufferings" (Heb. 2:10). He "learned" "obedience" "by the things which he suffered" (Heb. 5:8). He "overcame" and is "set down with" his "Father in His throne" (Rev. 3:21). He is in the "image of God" (Col. 1:15, Heb. 1:3, II Cor. 4:4). He is our "forerunner" passed into the holiest place (Heb. 6:20) and has the fullness of God (Col. 1:19), who is his "head" (I Cor. 11:3), dwelling IN him. He is the pioneer, the first person to go a new way (Heb. 2:10), who has overcome to become what God intended him to be and intends us to be. He "suffered for us, leaving us an EXAMPLE, that" we "should follow his steps" (I Pet. 2:21). He told James and John that they would do what he was going to do on the cross: "drink of the cup" Jesus would "drink of" (Mt. 20:22,23). He blazed a trail for us to follow so we can be in God's image and have God's fullness dwell in us and be "joint-heirs with Christ" (Rom. 8:17) crowned with honor and glory, following our "forerunner" (Heb. 6:20) into the holiest place. We now should live and behave as Jesus did, "walk even as he [Jesus] walked" (I Jn. 2:6).

You might think that Jesus was partly divine and had an advantage we do not have. That is definitely not the case. He would not expect us to do what he did if he had had an unfair advantage; and we should not expect it either. The idea that Jesus was equipped differently than we are is a myth that can keep us from understanding Jesus and from knowing God's opportunity in His kingdom. It would cause us to believe that God's purpose to change us from glory to glory by Jesus' Spirit (II Cor. 3:18) is impossible for us.

We can expect God to work with us through Jesus the same way He worked with our Lord. And we can expect the same results, that we be changed into the image of Christ which is the image of God. The creation is waiting expectantly for the "manifestation of the sons of God" (Rom. 8:19). We can refuse the delusional gospel and ungodly churches and their heresies, or we can stay with the many who make what Jesus actually did of no value and we mislead others.

We note here that the first verses of John are translated to say twice that the "word" was with God and once that the "word" was God. Actually, the manuscript says twice that the "word" was **toward** (Greek *pros*) "the God." The preposition *pros* indicates interaction between "the God" and the "word" and that the two were not the same. And John did not write that powerful wrong thought that the "Word was God" (Jn. 1:1): correct translations say either that the "word" was godly or divine or that the "word" was a god (See Vincent's *Word Studies in the New Testament* or *Young's Concise Critical Bible Commentary*). Though the manuscript does **not** say that the "word" was "**the** God," verses 1 and 2 say "the word" was "with [toward] **the** God." The "word" was a god or was godly; but the word was toward (not the K.J.V. "with") "the God."

Not only was Jesus not God, Jesus was not the Creator; but all things came into being through him and not the K.J.V.'s "made by him" (Jn. 1:3,10). Col. 1:16 should say "in him [Greek *en* for *in*] all things were created" instead of the K.J.V. "by him." The last of Col. 1:16 should say "through [Gr. *di*] him and unto [Gr. *eis*] him" rather than the K.J.V. "by him and for him." Eph. 2:10 says we are "created in Christ" by God's workmanship. Eph. 3:9 in the K.J.V. says God created "all things by Jesus Christ" but should say "through." The "by whom He also made the worlds" of the K.J.V. Heb. 1:2 should be "through whom also He made the ages." Eph. 2:10 is the only correct K.J.V. translation out of the seven.

Jesus is "the firstborn among many brethren" (Rom. 8:29), the "firstborn of every creature" (Col. 1:15) and the "firstborn from the dead" (Col. 1:18). We are the second born. Jesus is our "forerunner" (Heb. 6:20) and we are his after runners. Jesus is our pioneer leader (Heb. 2:10) and shepherd and lord and brother who is actively with us always. He is the firstborn of many brethren (Rom. 8:29): we are his brethren and are to be joint-heirs with him (Rom. 8:17). He is "the firstborn of every creature" (Col. 1:15) and, like us, is a creature or creation of God. He is a man (I Tim. 2:5) and is a soul (Mt. 26:38, Acts 2:27). He receives from God "dominion, and glory and the kingdom" (Dan. 7:13,14) which shall later be given to "the people of the saints of the Most High" (Dan. 7:27), Jesus' brethren.

105

We can be his followers, his sheep, his servants or voluntary slaves, his body, those who hear his voice and will not follow a stranger, those undergoing metamorphosis from glory to glory into his likeness, those having their minds renewed, holy and royal priests, those dwelling in Jesus with him dwelling in us, and members one of another among authentic brethren and those who live the way Jesus did and who are his active body. That is what the kingdom of God and salvation are about. The polluted church is an insult to the kingdom of God.

We are to be "the light of the world" (Mt. 5:14) because he is the "light of the world" (Jn. 8:12); and he in us can give light where and as he wishes if we quit doing our wills and do his. We need to let him "build" his "church" (Mt. 16:18) and to quit doing what our natural minds have decided to be good for Jesus.

God has great adventure for each of us as we live to Jesus and participate in the kingdom of God. That is the opportunity of the gospel of the kingdom of God. It is beyond description and the adventure is different for each of us. We, like Jesus, will be made perfect (perfected) through sufferings (Heb. 2:10) and will learn obedience through the things we suffer (Heb. 5:8). We will go through a metamorphosis of our minds (Rom. 12:2) and beings (II Cor. 3:18). We will suffer with him and become joint-heirs with him (Rom. 8:17). We will "work out" our "own salvation with fear and trembling" (Phil. 2:12). We will sit down in his throne with him if we are overcoming as he also overcame and sat down with God in His throne (Rev. 3:21). It is for now. It is full of challenges and changes. The kingdom of God is at hand and everyone should be pressing into it (Lk. 16:16). We need to not be stupid and "neglect so great salvation" (Heb. 2:3). Will we respond to God or be stupid?

8

Remarks

There was a time when the Israelites were saved from being slaves to the Egyptians. God took them into a desert and made them hunger, fed them, fought for them, led them, revealed His power and taught them for 40 years so they would "know that man does not live by bread alone, but by every word that proceeds out of the mouth of the LORD does man live" (Deut. 8:3).

God had offered to be speaking to each of them with their being a kingdom of priests (Ex. 19:5,6). They did not believe that men are to live by God's "every word" and God's deal, His Covenant. They wanted to have their own way and not be priests or God's kingdom. So God took them to the desert for 40 years and made them totally dependent on Him.

They had stopped their ears. They demanded that Moses speak to them for God and that God not speak to them directly so that they would not die (Ex. 20:19). They saw death rather than life (living by every precious word of God) as being the result of God speaking to them. They did not trust God and they did not want to have Him taking away their living to what they thought was their independence but what was really their being slaves to the desires of their bodies and immature minds (Eph. 2:3) that were making them stupid. They were like children who think they know better than their parents and then live in stupidity. They demanded separation from God. God wants us to grow up.

God gave them laws to tell them what to do and what not to do. He did not require that they hear or "obey His voice." He gave them law because "by the law is the knowledge [way of recognizing] of sin" (Rom. 3:20). But law can never produce righteousness (Rom. 3:20). It was a ministration of condemnation and death (II Cor. 3:7,9) that had them trying to be right but finding that they could not sustain doing so (Acts 15:10), which is why God gave them the laws and let them try to be righteous without His being **IN them** as their lives, directing, teaching them, maturing them and changing them to love and trust and grow from glory to glory (II Cor. 3:18) through different experiences. Some Pharisees and others tried hard to be righteous and became proud they were doing the parts of the law that **they recognized** as being important. They got approval from each other for doing what **they agreed** to be righteousness. They were deceived as are many church peoples who are righteous in their own eyes (self-righteous) by their efforts to please themselves, peers, and the world.

The Pharisees were meticulous about tithing and some other rules but "omitted" the more important parts of the law of "judgment, mercy [kindness] and faith [steadfastness, faithfulness]" (Mt. 23:23).

Major "Christianity" that we see today omits finding and entering the strait gate and narrow way, "walking" as Jesus "walked" always 24/7, obeying God's voice, men maintaining a good conscience toward God, following and obeying the Shepherd, loving one another, laying down one's life for another person, submitting to one another in the fear of God, having churches in which all members are active ministering priests having different ministries and equal care for each other, refusing any voice but the Shepherd's, individuals taking in the homeless and taking care of those in prison and sick and feeding the hungry and clothing the naked, pressing into the kingdom (rule) of God, "teaching" people "to observe all things whatsoever" Jesus "commanded" (Mt, 28:20), treating each other as parts of Jesus, being responsible for what one believes, trying the spirits and proving all things, and much else. Such "Christianity" rejects authentic Christianity.

It omits Christianity. Its people reject Christ while saying they are doing his will and keeping his commandments.

For authentic Christians who are "doers of the word, and not hearers only, deceiving" their "own selves" (Ja. 1:22), righteousness is to be rightly related to Jesus and God. It is a **relationship** in which we press into God's kingdom or rule (Lk. 16:16) and faithfully try to please Jesus and God directly by knowing and doing the will of God and participating with Him. It is something we do; but it is not something we do to please ourselves except as we are pleased to please God. Our faith sometimes shows by what we do (Ja. 2:18). It is not that we have faith in God being real or Jesus being His Son: it is that we are individually hearing and being faithful to Jesus and God. It is participation with God and Jesus (Jn. 17:21,23) and those who love truth and "walk in the light" (I Jn. 1:3,5,7). Jesus is the savior of those who are obeying him (Heb. 5.9).

The "ministration of condemnation" (II Cor. 3:9) is over for Christians (Rom. 8:1). Both God and men know that men have to overcome sinfulness that men by God's will have; and that sin can only be eliminated by their being transformed from glory to glory and inhabited by Jesus and God when they press into being ruled by God in His kingdom and being "led by the Spirit of God" (Rom. 8:14, Gal. 5:16). They know that God has always "forgiven" or sent away sins for those who truly repented so that they were changed people (that is true now and has never changed since the beginning of time); and that a changed character is what God wants and what men should want. They know that they have responsibility to do what is right and control themselves to cease to do wrong. When they know they need metamorphosis and need Jesus in them, blood is getting to their brains and they are truly wise.

There is no "condemnation to them which are in Christ Jesus" (Rom.8:1). God has said that under the New Covenant He will "be merciful to" our "unrighteousness and" our "sins and" "iniquities will" He "remember no more" (Heb. 8:12). He gives grace and mercy to those who will receive His mercy.

God has gotten out of the business of putting men under condemnation and pointing out their failures if they will be trying to please Him by individually following and hearing Jesus and doing His will and commandments. Paul said he did not evaluate his performance (I Cor. 4:3) but left that to the true Judge, God; although he said to "examine yourselves whether you be in the faith" (II Cor. 13:5), whether you are living to Jesus. Our new "born again" relationship of dwelling in Jesus 24/7 makes it so that we cannot continue to sin and do not want sin. We live to Jesus and not to ourselves (II Cor. 5:15). It is a totally new and different, exciting way of life.

We are not trying to be good and so feel good about ourselves. We are trying to obey God and do His will; and that causes us to be parts of Jesus doing good.

A great and elusive secret was uttered by Jesus: "No one is good but One, that is, God" (Mt. 19:17). James wrote: "Every good gift and every perfect gift is from above, and comes down from the Father of lights..." (Ja. 1:17).

God has a monopoly on goodness (Godness). He also is love (I Jn. 4: 8,16). He has a monopoly on love also. Any goodness or unselfish love (Gr. *agape*) that a person has is supplied by God; and few people realize that. Most people think they can have unselfish love and be good because of their own abilities. They cannot. Without God, it is impossible to do anything from unselfish love. God can remove unselfish love from you; and then you will know that Mt. 19:16 and Ja. 1:17 are absolutely true. Great things happen when we host God to live in and through us. He at times, though, lives through people when they do not know or acknowledge Him or intend to obey Him. He does more when His people are trying to obey Him as His kingdom.

Men have tried to please God with burnt sacrifices and self-righteous deeds. God is unimpressed. We need to give up and accept that righteousness comes by our dying to self, being subject to God, and our being faithful to and trusting God and His goodness the same as it did for Abraham. It is by faith that is faithfulness. It is an activity that we engage in. It is living by Christ IN us. It is righteousness by faithfulness to God and not to men or a church group or even our own selves (I Cor. 4:3,4).

We lose independence so we can be joined to God and participate where there is freedom and everything that is good for us. We get out of spiritual sewage to quit polluting ourselves and live in truth, joy, love, righteousness, unfading security and greater and greater life in fellowship and participation with the real God Himself and His Son.

To do these things we must "be endued with power from on high" that Jesus spoke of as "the promise of" his "Father" that Jesus would send (Lk. 24:49), the Holy Spirit or "Spirit or truth" that Jesus said was "**dwelling with**" the disciples and would be "**IN**" them (Jn. 14:17). You must "be baptized with the Holy Ghost" (Acts 1:5) and "receive power" that Jesus said we would receive "after that the Holy Ghost is come upon" us (Acts. 1:8). It is absolutely a prerequisite to our being spiritual and growing as God has provided for us. It is not optional though nearly half of Christians have not availed themselves of surrendering to Jesus and letting the Spirit come IN them as a permanent resident doing God's will in them.

The false gospel says God is mean, selfish and easily offended, a failure as a planner, incapable of "forgiving" sins unless He gets natural blood, and has a mess on His hands for which He did not plan when He caused the birth of billions of souls that did not know or believe in Him and had no reason to obey Him and be in His kingdom. It says that He had a problem with His revengefulness that He solved by taking out His anger on His Son who "bore" the penalty of our sins on the cross. It says He did not forgive our sins but transferred the penalty of sins to someone who was innocent. It claims that men are considered righteous by Him if they believe He is a bad person with hate and anger such that He has provided never ending torture for whoever does not believe that He is a monster having His anger deleted by killing His Son on a cross.

We must choose. We are responsible for what we believe and for what we do or neglect to do. We can live in light and truth and help others to do the same. We can choose to live in fables and to men, men's organizations, and ourselves. We can be smart or stupid. God's way is available and many other ways are present to temp us. The choice is ours.

There are "Christians" who are confident, lukewarm and nauseating to Jesus. They are those who are in Jesus who will be vomited out of his mouth (Rev. 3:16,17). There are the "many" who take the wide gate and broad way that lead to destruction and will depart from Jesus and weep and gnash their teeth as "workers of iniquity" (Lk. 13:24-28, Mt. 7:13). There are those who know the will of Jesus and do not do it and will weep and gnash their teeth in outer darkness (Mt. 25:26-30). There are "many" who will confidently claim to Jesus that they have, in his name, cast out demons and prophesied and done wonderful works and will be told that Jesus never knew them and to depart from him (Mt. 7:22,23). Some are not taking in strangers and taking care of the sick and those in prison (government facilities or mental fears and false understandings) and feeding and giving drink to those in need and clothing them; and these will go into fire prepared for the devil and his messengers (Mt. 25: 41-46; I Tim. 5:10). The penalties that "Christians" and other men will suffer for being stubborn and

111

stupid will do their work and convince men to change their thinking the same as a little disciplining will drive foolishness from a child. That is how God deals with stubbornness and stupidity without taking away a person's free will.

The aim of this book has been to expose and destroy false teachings that have prevented men from knowing Christ and God and to present truth that will enable people to live victoriously to Christ. It tries to point the way. Judge it and "hold fast that which is good" (I Thes. 5:21). Only God can reveal truth. He will correct and expand what is written here as He wishes. We "know nothing yet as" we "ought" (I Cor. 8:2); we "know in part and we prophesy in part" (I Cor. 13: 9,12). The Holy Spirit, Jesus' Spirit, is perfecting us (II Cor. 3:18). He has much, much more to be revealing to us. He is the One sent to "guide" us "into all truth" (Jn. 16:13) and he "is teaching" us "of all things" (I Jn. 2:27). We are at a starting point when we begin to worship in spirit and truth and honor God as God and refuse the "bugs." We need to responsibly walk with God, knowing and doing His will.

The scriptures contain "great and precious promises that by these you might be partakers of the divine nature" (II Pet. 1:4). They can, when they are rightly translated and made alive by the Spirit, "make you wise unto salvation" (II Tim. 3:15). The Holy Spirit has been sent to lead each of us into all truth. Jesus is God's Shepherd whose "voice" should lead each of us. Authentic church is to be treasured and sought: from phony church and phony gospel, we should flee.

The question for each of us is one that Pilate asked: "What shall I do then with Jesus which is called Christ?" (Lk. 27:22). Will I "neglect so great salvation" (Heb. 2:3)? Will I change my life so I can serve God and be moved and led by God such that I am in the born again activity (Jn. 3:8) directed by God 24/7? Will I require authentic church or stay where I am not being a participating priest of God 24/7 participating with other of God's priests and being parts one of another? Will I seek until I am finding the strait gate and narrow way that lead to life and not to destruction? Will I meet with others and seek real worship in spirit and truth and accept nothing less? Will I press into God's kingdom?

Will I give up friends, false church, clubs, hobbies, jobs, wealth, businesses and anything else that interferes with my doing what Jesus has for me to do (Mt. 19:29, Lk.14:33)? Will I refuse and run from men usurping Jesus and claiming to be my spiritual rulers, fathers or intermediaries between God and myself? Will I refuse to obey any voice but that of the Shepherd? Will I submit to listen to authentic Christians in the fear of God? Will I look for and refuse and flee from false prophets? Will I be a doer of the Word or just a hearer deceiving myself? Will I live in truth? Will I be responsible for what I believe?

God has opened the way into His control or kingdom and the New Covenant where we can participate with Him and know Him and His Son and be changed into His likeness, the likeness of Christ. That is **the** good news or gospel of the kingdom of God. We understand more and more as (1) we "continue in" participation in doing Jesus' word (Jn. 8:31,32; II Cor. 3:18), and as (2) Jesus comes in our presence when any 2 or 3 or more are gathered in his name anywhere they are, and (3) when we hear Jesus and when his anointing comes on us and (4) when we use God's "great and precious promises" and (5) when God in us is willing and doing His good pleasure and we are led by him and are doing the will and word of God. False church is destructive and is Christ's and our enemy. Real church will attract authentic people and be used greatly by Jesus as his body.

God's offer is on the table. This book has tried to show God's word as it is and show the futility in entering imaginations that substitute for God's word and are embraced by the many who are taking the wide path that leads to destruction.

We have the opportunity to persevere and be being rewarded with treasures inexpressible. There are "exceeding great and precious promises: that by these you might be partakers of the divine nature, having escaped the corruption that is in the world through lust" (II Pet. 1:4). "All things" are working "together for good to them who love God [those obeying and living to God], to them who are called according to His purpose" (Rom. 8:28). God is doing a "good work" in you, and He will not quit (Phil. 1:6).

If we will give up the "bugs," "viruses" and "worms," in Christian living and thought, we can see and participate in Christ and God's kingdom. Man-organized churches keep men from Jesus and do not have authentic worship, worship in spirit and truth. If we do not meticulously give up the "bugs," "viruses" and

113

"worms," we will not know Christ and his power in us and we will not be participating in the kingdom of God and growing into the likeness of Jesus, the likeness of God. We will be being destroyed.

But if we choose to be responsible and live to God as His children and born again brethren and members of Jesus's body and church, our future is guaranteed to be greater and greater, from glory to glory.